CELEBRATE 2000!

Celebrate 2000!
A THREE-YEAR READER
Reflections on Jesus, the Holy Spirit, and the Father

POPE JOHN PAUL II

Selected and Arranged by
Paul Thigpen

CHARIS

Servant Publications
Ann Arbor, Michigan

Charis Books is an imprint of Servant Publications especially designed to serve Roman Catholics.

All selections have been taken from the official Vatican translation of papal documents. Some are from encyclicals and apostolic letters published in the United States by Pauline Books & Media. Other texts appeared originally in the official Vatican newspaper, *L'Osservatore Romano* (English edition, Via del Pellegrino, 00120 Vatican City, Europe). They were reprinted in *The Pope Speaks*, a bimonthly periodical published by *Our Sunday Visitor* (200 Noll Plaza, Huntington, IN 46750). Used by permission. All rights reserved.

Published by Servant Publications
P.O. Box 8617
Ann Arbor, Michigan 48107

96 97 98 99 00 10 9 8 7 6 5 4 3

Printed in the United States of America
ISBN 0-89283-956-2

Library of Congress Cataloging-in-Publication Data

John Paul II, Pope
 [Selections. English. 1996]
 Celebrate 2000! : a three year reader : reflections on Jesus, the Holy Spirit, and the Father / Pope John Paul II : selected and arranged by Paul Thigpen.
   p. cm.
 "This book contains the complete text of the apostolic letter, The coming of the third millenium." —CIP galley.
 Includes bibliographical references (p.).
 ISBN 0-89283-956-2
 1. Trinity—Prayer-books and devotions—English. 2. Spiritual life—Catholic Church—Prayer-books and devotions—English. 3. Catholic Church—Prayer-books and devotions—English. 4. Two thousand, A.D. 5. Devotional calendars. I. Catholic Church. Pope (1978-   : John Paul II). Tertio millennio adveniente. English. 1996. II. Title.
BT111.2.J64213 1996
248.4'82—dc20   96-7610
                                                                CIP

CONTENTS

An Invitation
to Celebrate

They call it "the zero effect."

Historians have noted that many people grow increasingly anxious as they approach years ending in zero, such as 1980 or 1990. Perhaps the zero years are fearful because they suggest to us that one era is ending and another, yet unknown, is beginning. In any case, the more zeros there are, the greater the anxiety that people feel. So tension rises at the end of a decade; more so at the end of a century; and most of all at the end of a millennium.

Talk about the end of the world is common at these times, especially when the year has more than one zero. According to some reports, as the first millennium of Christian history drew to a close many folks even grew hysterical. They were convinced that Christ would return to judge the world at the stroke of midnight on January first of the year 1000.

Now the second millennium is ending, an extraordinary "three-zero" year is coming once again—and not surprisingly, the doomsday predictions are being resurrected. Some Christians speak of living in the last days, in the "Omega generation." Others swap rumors about Marian apparitions hinting that the end is near. Even in non-Christian circles, speculation about the impending close of history has been fed by predictions from such diverse sources as an ancient Mayan calendar stone, the sixteenth-century writer Nostradamus, the twentieth-century psychic Edgar Cayce, and alleged recent contacts with extraterrestrial visitors.

In the midst of these troubled and troubling voices, a calmer, more optimistic voice calls out to focus attention on the year 2000. While others cry, "Repent—for the end is near," Pope John Paul II declares, "Repent—for a new beginning has come!" While others prepare for doomsday, he calls the Church and indeed the whole world to prepare instead for the third millennium, with a burning hope that God the Father, through Christ and His Spirit, is still at work to renew His beloved creation.

The future, insists the Pope, holds remarkable possibilities for those who open themselves to the Holy Spirit's intentions. The year 2000 is actually a door of divine grace. If we will cross this "threshold of hope" into God's purposes, he says, we can take part in a "new springtime" that heralds the transformation of ourselves, our Church, our nation, and our entire planet.

Confident in this hope, Pope John Paul II has announced that the Church will observe the year 2000 as a "Great Jubilee": a particular year of God's favor, a sign of His unfailing love, a season to remember and rejoice that two millennia ago, Christ came to set us free from the bonds of sin. Like all Jubilee years, it will be, he says, "a year of the remission of sins and of the punishments due them, a year of reconciliation between disputing parties, a year of manifold conversions and of sacramental and extra-sacramental penance." The Pope wants the entire year to be celebrated exuberantly as an unprecedented birthday party for Jesus—and the whole world is invited to come. But we can't show up at a birthday party dirty-faced, ragged, and empty-handed. We have to get ourselves ready to honor the Lord and to celebrate His coming. No doubt our Heavenly Father loves us as we are, spiritual urchins though we may be. Yet He loves us too much to let us remain as we are. For that reason, the Pope calls us to make preparations.

The whole Christian community should enjoy the Great Jubilee as a feast that will nourish our spirits, put a song in our hearts, and send us out into the world dancing. Before that can happen for most of us, however, we have some work to do. It's time to give our souls a bath, to dress in our spiritual best, and to take in our hands the gift of our will, wrapped in a fervent desire to see Christ's Kingdom come.

To help us get ready for this grand party, Pope John Paul II has outlined a strategy in his apostolic letter of November 10, 1994, entitled "As the Third Millennium Draws Near." There, he notes that the Second Vatican Council, subsequent Church synods, holy years, and papal teachings have all played their part in moving the Church toward the Jubilee. But in these last few years of the fading second millennium, the Church needs a specific program of practical initiatives designed to prepare us for the dawning third millennium.

The Pope calls for preparations to take two phases. The first phase, extending through 1996, is to make Christians aware of the value and meaning of the Jubilee year. The second phase—consisting of the years 1997, 1998, and 1999—is intended to turn the Church's attention to God Himself, to help us grow deeper in our knowledge of Him, our love for Him, our joy in Him. Each of these years is to be devoted to reflection on a particular Person within the Holy Trinity: Father, Son, and Holy Spirit.

The order in which we're called to meditate on the three Persons of God in these years reflects, at least in one sense, the order in which we encounter them in human history and in our personal lives. The first year, 1997, is intended to center on God the Son, Jesus Christ—the One whose glorious invasion of history and of our lives first allowed us to encounter God face-to-face. In 1998, we turn our attention to God the Holy Spirit, Love Himself, the Person sent by Christ to set ablaze the hearts of His disciples and, by their hands, to turn the world upside down. In the Spirit's coming at Pentecost, the Church has encountered God as the One who lives in us and through us.

Finally, in the year 1999, we are to focus on God the Father. The Son of God and the Spirit of God came precisely for this reason: to turn our hearts toward the Father, to restore our friendship with Him, to bring us back to His loving embrace. We center on Him in this last year because He Himself is our final destination, the One we will encounter at last as the source of all things and the fulfillment of all things.

In each year, Pope John Paul suggests, we should allow our meditation on a Person of the Holy Trinity to lead us to reflect as well on certain related themes. Faith, hope, and love—the three "theological virtues," as they have been called—provide one such set of themes. As we turn our souls toward Christ, we should ponder the meaning of faith in Him. As we look to the Holy Spirit, we should dwell on the meaning of the hope He brings. And as we seek out God the Father, who loved the world into being, we should delve deeply into the meaning of this love.

The Pope notes that other themes fall naturally into the focus of meditation for each of the three years. Concerns about ecumenism, for example, easily arise when we begin to think of Christ and of all those who call themselves by His name. Thoughts about the nature of the Church accompany thoughts about the Holy Spirit, who fills and energizes the Church. Reflection on God the Father, who created all people, presses us to consider as well our role in serving the world beyond the Church.

Finally, in his apostolic letter the Pope calls all Christians to take part in the Jubilee preparations. "Everyone," he urges, "is asked to do as much as possible to ensure that the great challenge of the Year 2000 is not overlooked, for this challenge certainly involves a special grace of the Lord for the Church and for the whole of humanity." This book is an effort to heed that call, to make some small contribution to the Church's preparation for that year of divine favor. What better way could there be to encourage God's people to nourish themselves on these vital themes than to offer Pope John Paul II's own profound reflections as food for thought?

The structure of this book, which is a compilation

of brief excerpts from the Holy Father's extensive written works, follows his strategy for preparation. The first major section focuses on God the Son, on the virtue of faith, on Mary as a model of faith, and on related issues such as ecumenism, catechesis, spiritual disciplines, and the Scriptures. The second major section centers on God the Holy Spirit, on the virtue of hope, on Mary as a model of hope, and on associated topics such as the nature of the Church and the Kingdom of God, the gifts of the Spirit, and evangelism. The last major section dwells on God the Father, the virtue of love (or charity), Mary as a model of love, and themes such as sexuality, the family, social action, interreligious dialogue, and the sanctity of life.

The goal here, of course, is not simply meditation, but transformation. The Pope has called us to look long and hard at God because to know God truly is to love Him, and to love Him truly is to become like Him. St. Paul spoke of the process long ago: "We all,... beholding the glory of the Lord, are being changed into his likeness" (2 Cor 3:18). St. John promised that "we shall be like [God]" when we "see him as he is"; and even the hope of seeing Him purifies us (see 1 John 3:2-3). In setting our minds on the Lord during these three years, then, we're bathing and dressing our souls, getting ready for Jesus' grand birthday party, where the gift we bring will be ourselves.

When we survey the multitude of writings from which these passages are drawn, we must marvel not only at the remarkable volume of this shepherd's labors, but also at their inner consistency, at the systematic and comprehensive quality of thought he has offered the Church in our day. The Great Jubilee of 2000, he has said, is the key to the meaning of his pontificate. As we put together a total picture of his work, we discover that from the earliest days of his reign, that pivotal year has appeared repeatedly in his thinking as an organizing principle. The bright future for which 2000 is the threshold provides the hope upon which all his teachings ultimately converge.

Let the doomsayers prophesy as they will. In Pope John Paul II, we encounter an alternative vision of compelling beauty. Here is a wise and tireless man who has gladly spent his life to paint a full, richly detailed portrait of God the Father, God the Son, and God the Holy Spirit—so that the whole world might behold and fall deeply in love with the One who calls us to Himself at the dawn of the Third Millennium.

—Paul Thigpen

How to Use This Book

In the apostolic letter *Tertio Millennio Adveniente*, Pope John Paul II calls on Christians to prepare themselves for the Jubilee year 2000 by reflecting prayerfully on the nature of God—Father, Son, and Holy Spirit—and on the fundamental themes of the Christian life. The selections from the Pope's writings and addresses included in this book have been arranged according to the strategy for reflection he offered in the apostolic letter (which appears in full at the back of this book), with a focus on God the Son in 1997, God the Holy Spirit in 1998, and God the Father in 1999.

The result is a three-year reader that provides ample food for thought during this preparatory season. Fifty-two numbered readings are offered for each of the three years, one reading for each week of the year. The editor has carefully arranged the readings under topical headings. He has provided readers a few words of introduction to each major topic. We suggest that you read a selection at the beginning of each week and ponder its meaning. Allow it to challenge you throughout the following seven days. If you do, by the end of these three years you will no doubt have found the pope's words to be a rich source of insight, encouragement, and motivation to get ready for Jesus' great birthday celebration—and for the dawn of the Church's third millennium.

Abbreviations used in Sources

CA   *Centesimus Annus*
CL   *Christifideles Laici*
CT   *Catechesi Tradendae*
DC   *Dominicae Cenae*
DM   *Dives in Misericordia*
DV   *Dominum et Vivificantem*
EV   *Evangelium Vitae*
FC   *Familiaris Consortio*
LE   *Laborem Exercens*
MD   *Mulieris Dignitatem*
NAB   *New American Bible*
NE   *Negotiation*
OR   *L'Osservatore Romano* (followed by date and page)
PDV   *Pastores Dabo Vobis*
RH   *Redemptor Hominis*
RM   *Redemptoris Missio*
RMa   *Redemptoris Mater*
RP   *Reconciliato et Paenitentia*
SC   *Sapientia Christiana*
SRS   *Sollicitudo Rei Socialis*
TMA   *Tertio Millennio Adveniente*
TPS   *The Pope Speaks* (followed by volume/number, year, pages)
VS   *Veritatis Splendor*

1997

YEAR ONE OF PREPARATION:
Encountering God the Son

JESUS CHRIST, THE SON OF GOD

Jesus Christ is the Way, the Truth, and the Life; no one comes to the Father except through Him (see John 14:6). To reach the Father as our destination, we must begin with the Son, whose coming has made it possible to be reconciled to God and to live in faith and holiness.

THE WEEK OF JANUARY 5, 1997

1. CHRIST—GOD'S SEARCH FOR MAN

Jesus does not... merely speak in the name of God like the Prophets, but He is God Himself speaking in His Eternal Word Made Flesh. Here we touch upon the essential point by which Christianity differs from all other religions, by which man's search for God has been expressed from earliest times. Christianity has its starting point in the Incarnation of the Word.

Here, it is not simply a case of man seeking God, but of God who comes in Person to speak to man of Himself and to show him the path by which He may be reached. This is what is proclaimed in... John's Gospel: "No one has ever seen God; the only Son, who is in the bosom of the Father, he has made him known" (Jn 1:18). The Incarnate Word is thus the fulfillment of the yearning present in all the religions of mankind: this fulfillment is brought about by God Himself and transcends all human expectations. It is the mystery of grace. [TMA n. 6]

THE WEEK OF JANUARY 12, 1997

2. GOD SEEKS US OUT IN CHRIST

In Jesus Christ God not only speaks to man but also seeks him out. The Incarnation of the Son of God attests that God goes in search of man. Jesus speaks of this search as the finding of a lost sheep (see Luke 15:1-7).

It is a search which begins in the heart of God and culminates in the Incarnation of the Word. If God goes in search of man, created in His own image and likeness, He does so because He loves him eternally in the Word, and wishes to raise him in Christ to the dignity of an adoptive son. God therefore goes in search of man, who is His special possession in a way unlike any other creature. Man is God's possession by virtue of a choice made in love: God seeks man out, moved by His fatherly heart.

Why does God seek man out? Because man has turned away from Him, hiding himself as Adam did among the trees of the Garden of Eden (see Genesis 3:8-10). Man allowed himself to be led astray by the enemy of God (see Genesis 3:13). Satan deceived man, persuading him that he too was a god, that he, like God, was capable of knowing good and evil, ruling the world according to his own will without having to take into account the divine will (see Genesis 3:5).

Going in search of man through His Son, God wishes to persuade man to abandon the paths of evil which lead him farther and farther afield. Making him abandon those paths means making man understand that he is taking the wrong path; it means overcoming the evil which is everywhere found in human history. Overcoming evil: this is the meaning of the Redemption.

This is brought about in the sacrifice of Christ, by which man redeems the debt of sin and is reconciled to God. The Son of God became man, taking a body and soul in the womb of the Virgin, precisely for this reason: to become the perfect redeeming sacrifice. The religion of the Incarnation is the religion of the world's Redemption through the sacrifice of Christ, wherein lies victory over evil, over sin, and over death itself. Accepting death on the Cross, Christ at the same time reveals and gives life, because He rises again and death no longer has power over Him. [TMA n. 7]

THE WEEK OF JANUARY 19, 1997

3. THE TRUTH OF CHRIST BRINGS FREEDOM

Jesus Christ meets the man of every age, including our own, with the same words: "You will know the truth, and the truth will make you free" (Jn 8:32). These words contain both a fundamental require- ment and a warning: the requirement of an honest relationship with regard to truth as a condition for authentic freedom, and the warning to avoid every kind of illusory freedom,... every freedom that fails to enter into the whole truth about man and the world.

Today also, even after two thousand years, we see Christ as the One who brings man freedom based on truth—frees man from what curtails, diminishes, and as it were breaks off this freedom at its root, in man's soul, his heart, and his conscience. [RH n. 12]

THE WEEK OF JANUARY 26, 1997

4. CHRIST OFFERS A FULL LIFE

Jesus came to provide the ultimate answer to the yearning for life and for the infinite which His Heavenly Father had poured into our hearts when He created us. At the climax of revelation, the incar- nate Word [Christ] proclaims, "I am... the Life" (Jn 14:6), and "I came that they might have life" (Jn 10:10).

But what life? Jesus' intention was clear: the very life of God, which surpasses all the possible aspirations of the human heart (see 1 Corinthians 2:9). The fact is that through the grace of Baptism we are already God's children (see 1 John 3:1-2).

Our daily experience tells us that life is marked by sin and threatened by death, despite the desire for good which beats in our hearts and the desire for life which courses through our veins. However little heed we pay to ourselves and to the frustrations which life brings us, we discover that everything within us impels us to transcend ourselves, urges us to overcome the temptation of superficiality or despair. It is then that human beings are called to become disciples of that other One who infinitely transcends them, in order to enter at last into true life....

Left to ourselves, we could never achieve the ends for which we have been created. Within us there is a promise which we find we are incapable of attaining. But the Son of God who came among us has given us His personal assurance: "I am the Way, and the Truth, and the Life" (Jn 14:6). As St. Augustine so strikingly phrased it, Christ "wishes to create a place in which it is possible for all people to find true life." This "place" is His Body and His Spirit, in which the whole of human life, redeemed and forgiven, is renewed and made divine. [TPS 38/1, 1993, 40-41]

THE WEEK OF FEBRUARY 2, 1997

5. CHRIST, FOCUS OF THE CHURCH'S MISSION

The Church's fundamental function in every age, and particularly in ours, is to direct man's gaze, to point the awareness and experience of the whole of humanity, toward the mystery of God, to help all men to be familiar with the profundity of the Redemption taking place in Christ Jesus.... In Christ and through Christ God has revealed Himself fully to mankind and has definitively drawn close to it; at the same time, in Christ and through Christ man has acquired full awareness of his dignity, of the heights to which he is raised, of the surpassing worth of his own humanity, and of the meaning of his existence. All of us who are Christ's followers must therefore meet and unite around Him. [RH n. 10-11]

THE WEEK OF FEBRUARY 9, 1997

6. JESUS CHRIST IS THE ONLY SAVIOR

The Church's universal mission is born of faith in Jesus Christ.... It is only in faith that the Church's mission can be understood and only in faith that it finds its basis.

Nevertheless... as a result of the changes which have taken place in modern times and the spread of new theological ideas, some people wonder: Is missionary work among non-Christians still relevant? Has it not been replaced by interreligious dialogue? Is not human development an adequate goal of the Church's mission? Does not respect for conscience and for freedom exclude all efforts at conversion? Is it not possible to attain salvation in any religion? Why then should there be missionary activity?

If we go back to the beginnings of the Church, we find a clear affirmation that Christ is the one Savior of all, the only one able to reveal God and to lead to God. In reply to the Jewish religious authorities who question the apostles about the healing of the lame man, Peter says: "By the name of Jesus Christ of Nazareth whom you crucified, whom God raised from the dead, by him this man is standing before you well.... And there is salvation in no one else, for there is no other name under heaven given among men by which we must be saved" (Acts 4:10-12). This statement, which was made to the Sanhedrin, has a universal value, since for all people—Jews and Gentiles alike—salvation can only come from Jesus Christ.

The universality of this salvation in Christ is asserted throughout the New Testament. St. Paul acknowledges the risen Christ as the Lord. He writes: "Although there may be so-called gods in heaven or on earth—as indeed there are many 'gods' and many 'lords'—yet for us there is one God, the Father, from whom are all things and for whom we exist, and one Lord, Jesus Christ, from whom are all things and through whom we exist" (1 Cor 8:5-6). One God and one Lord are asserted by way of contrast to the multitude of "gods" and "lords" commonly accepted. Paul reacts against the polytheism of the religious environment of his time and emphasizes what is characteristic of the Christian faith: belief in one God and in one Lord sent by God....

In this definitive Word of His Revelation, God has made Himself known in the fullest possible way. He has revealed to humankind who He is. This definitive self-revelation of God is the fundamental reason why the Church is missionary by her very nature. She cannot do other than proclaim the Gospel, that is, the fullness of the truth which God has enabled us to know about Himself. [RM n. 4-5]

7. CHRIST, THE ONE MEDIATOR

Christ is the one mediator between God and human-kind: "For there is one God, and there is one media-tor between God and men, the man Christ Jesus, who gave himself as a ransom for all, the testimony to which was borne at the proper time. For this I was appointed a preacher and apostle (I am telling the truth, I am not lying), a teacher of the Gentiles in faith and truth" (1 Tm 2:5-7; see also Hebrews 4:14-16).

No one, therefore, can enter into communion with God except through Christ, by the working of the Holy Spirit. Christ's one, universal mediation, far from being an obstacle on the journey toward God, is the way established by God Himself, a fact of which Christ is fully aware. [RM 5]

8. CHRIST, THE TEACHER

The majesty of Christ the Teacher and the unique consistency and persuasiveness of His teaching can only be explained by the fact that His words, His parables, and His arguments are never separable from His life and His very being. Accordingly, the whole of Christ's life was a continual teaching. His silences, His miracles, His gestures, His prayer, His love for people, His special affection for the little and the poor, His acceptance of the total sacrifice on the cross for the redemption of the world, and His Resurrection are the actualization of His word and the fulfillment of revelation. Hence for Christians the crucifix is one of the most sublime and popular images of Christ the Teacher....

These considerations... all strengthen our fervor with regard to Christ, the Teacher who reveals God to man and man to himself, the Teacher who saves, sanctifies, and guides, who lives, who speaks, rouses, moves, redresses, judges, forgives, and goes with us day by day on the path of history, the Teacher who comes and will come in glory. [CT n. 9]

9. CHRIST IS SENDING YOU

To each one of you Christ says: "I am sending you."

Why is He sending you? Because men and women the world over... long for true liberation and fulfillment. The poor seek justice and solidarity; the oppressed demand freedom and dignity; the blind cry out for light and truth (see Luke 4:18). You are not being sent to proclaim some abstract truth. The Gospel is not a theory or an ideology! The Gospel is life!

Your task is to bear witness to this life: the life of God's adopted sons and daughters. Modern man, whether he knows it or not, urgently needs that life—just as 2,000 years ago humanity was in need of Christ's coming; just as people will always need Jesus Christ until the end of time.

Why do we need Him? Because Christ reveals the truth about man and man's life and destiny. He shows us our place before God, as creatures and sinners, as redeemed through His death and resurrection, as making our pilgrim way to the Father's house. He teaches the fundamental commandment of the love of God and love of neighbor. He insists that there cannot be justice, brotherhood, peace,

and solidarity without the Ten Commandments.…
[TPS 40/3, 1995, 165-6]

10. THE MESSAGE WE MUST PROCLAIM

The truth about man—which the modern world finds so hard to understand—is that we are made in the image and likeness of God Himself (see Genesis 1:27). Precisely in this fact, apart from any other consideration, lies the inalienable dignity of every human being, without exception, from the moment of conception until natural death. But what is even more difficult for contemporary culture to understand is that this dignity, already forged in the creative act of God, is raised immeasurably higher in the mystery of the Incarnation of the Son of God.

This is the message which you have to proclaim to the modern world: especially to the least fortunate, to the homeless and dispossessed, to the sick, the outcasts, to those who suffer at the hands of others. To each one you must say: Look to Jesus Christ in order to see who you really are in the eyes of God!

Increasing attention is being given to the cause of human dignity and human rights, and gradually these are being codified and included in legislation both at national and international levels. For this we should be grateful. But the effective and guaranteed observance of respect for human dignity and human rights will be impossible if individuals and communities do not overcome self-interest, fear, greed, and the thirst for power. And for this, man needs to be freed from the dominion of sin, through the life of grace: the grace of our Lord and Savior Jesus Christ.

Jesus says to you: "I am sending you to your families, to your parishes, to your movements and associations, to your countries, to ancient cultures and modern civilization, so that you will proclaim the dignity of every human being, as revealed by me, the Son of Man." If you defend the inalienable dignity of every human being, you will be revealing to the world the true face of Jesus Christ, who is one with every man, every woman, and every child, no matter how poor, no matter how weak or handicapped.

How does Jesus send you? He promises neither sword nor money nor power, nor any of the things which the means of social communications make attractive to people today. He gives you instead peace and truth. He sends you out with the powerful message of his Paschal Mystery, with the truth of His Cross and Resurrection. That is all He gives you, and that is all you need. [TPS 40/3, 1995, 166]

THE WEEK OF MARCH 16, 1997

11. SEEK JESUS ALWAYS!

Seek Jesus. Let your life be a continual, sincere search for the Savior, without ever tiring, without ever abandoning the undertaking; even though, at a certain moment, darkness should fall on your spirit, temptations beset you, and grief and incomprehension wring your heart. These are things which are part of life here below; they are inevitable, but they can also do good because they mature our spirit. You must never turn back, however, even if it should seem to you that the light of Christ, the "Light of the peoples," is fading. On the contrary, continue to seek with renewed faith and great generosity.

Deepen your knowledge of Jesus, listening to the word of the Ministers of the Lord, and reading some pages of the Gospel. Try to discover where He is, and you will be able to gather from everyone some detail that will indicate it to you, that will tell you where He lives. Ask souls that are meek, repentant, generous, humble, and hidden; ask your brothers, far and near, because you will find in everyone something that indicates Jesus to you. Ask, above all, your soul and your conscience, because they will be able to indicate to you, in an unmistakable way, a mark of His passing, a trace of His power and His love.

But ask humbly. That is, let your soul be ready to see, outside itself, those parts of His goodness that God has sown in creatures. To seek Him every day means possessing Him a little more every day, being admitted a little at a time to intimacy with Him; and then you will be able to understand better the sound of His voice, the meaning of His language, the reason for His coming to earth and for His sacrifice on the Cross. [OR 4-9-79, 4]

THE VIRTUE OF FAITH

When we encounter Christ, He calls us to respond with trust in His love and submission to His will—an act of faith based on God's perfect faithfulness.

THE WEEK OF MARCH 23, 1997

12. FAITH IN CHRIST

In Christ, religion is no longer a blind search for God (see Acts 17:27) but the response of faith to

God who reveals Himself. It is a response in which man speaks to God as his Creator and Father, a response made possible by that one Man... in whom God speaks to each individual person and by whom each individual person is enabled to respond to God.

What is more, in this Man all creation responds to God. Jesus Christ is the new beginning of everything. In Him all things come into their own; they are taken up and given back to the Creator from whom they first came. Christ is thus the fulfillment of the yearning of all the world's religions and, as such, He is their sole and definitive completion.

Just as God in Christ speaks to humanity of Himself, so in Christ all of humanity and the whole of creation speaks of itself to God—indeed, it gives itself to God. [TMA n. 6]

THE WEEK OF MARCH 30, 1997

13. BE FIRM IN YOUR FAITH

Be "firm in your faith" (see 1 Peter 5:9). Be so in the first place by means of thorough and gradual knowledge of the content of Christian doctrines. It is not enough to be Christians because of the Baptism received or because of the [historical and] social conditions in which you are born and live. As you grow in years and culture, new problems and new requirements of clarity come into consciousness. It is then necessary to set out in a responsible way in search of the motivations of your own Christian faith. If you do not become personally aware and do not have an adequate understanding of what must be believed and of the reasons for this faith, at a certain moment everything may inevitably collapse and be swept away, in spite of the good will of parents and educators.

Therefore, today is specially the time for study, meditation, and reflection. I say to you therefore: use your intelligence well, make an effort to reach correct and personal convictions, do not waste time, deepen the motives and foundations of faith in Christ and in the Church, so as to be firm now and in your future.

One is firm in the faith, furthermore, by means of prayer. St. Paul already recommended: "Pray constantly" (1 Thes 5:17). It is possible, in fact, to know Holy Scripture perfectly, it is possible to be learned in philosophy and in theology, yet not have faith, or fail in faith; because it is always God who calls first to know Him and love Him in the right way.

It is necessary, therefore, to be humble before the Almighty. It is necessary to maintain the sense of mystery, because there always remains the infinite between God and man. It is necessary to remember that before God and His Revelation it is not so much a question of understanding with one's own limited reason, but rather of loving.

For this reason Jesus said, "I thank Thee, Father, Lord of heaven and earth, that Thou hast hidden these things from the wise and understanding and revealed them to babes; yea, Father, for such was Thy gracious will" (Mt 11:25-26).[OR 4/2/79,4]

THE WEEK OF APRIL 6, 1997

14. FAITH: CERTAIN, STRONG, JOYFUL, ACTIVE
[May] your faith... be certain, that is, founded on the Word of God, on deep knowledge of the Gospel

message, and especially of the life, person, and work of Christ; and also on the interior witness of the Holy Spirit.

May your faith be strong; may it not hesitate, not waver, before the doubts, the uncertainties which philosophical systems or fashionable movements would like to suggest to you; may it not descend to compromises with certain concepts, which would like to present Christianity as a mere ideology at the same level as so many others, now outdated.

May your faith be joyful, because it is based on awareness of possessing a divine gift. When you pray and dialogue with God and when you converse with men, manifest the joy of this enviable possession.

Let your faith be active, let it manifest itself and take on concrete shape in laborious and generous charity toward brothers, who live crushed in sorrow and in need; let it be manifested in your serene adherence to the teaching of the truth; let it be expressed in your availability for all apostolic initiatives, in which you are called upon to participate for the expansion and the building up of the Kingdom of God. [OR 11/3/80, 3]

THE WEEK OF APRIL 13, 1997

15. FAITH AND REVEALED TRUTH

To believe means accepting the truth that comes from God with the whole conviction of the intellect, relying on the grace of the Holy Spirit "whom God has given to those who obey Him" (Acts 5:32): accepting what God has revealed, and what always reaches us by means of the Church in her living transmission, that is, in tradition. The organ of this tradition is the teaching of Peter and the Apostles and their successors.

To believe means accepting their witness in the Church, which guards this witness from generation to generation, and then—on the basis of this witness—to bear witness to the same truth, with the same certainty and interior conviction. [OR 5/5/80, 8]

THE WEEK OF APRIL 20, 1997

16. THE ANSWER OF FAITH

What is our faith?... Is this faith as univocal and clear as the faith confessed by Peter before the Sanhedrin? (See Acts 5:17-42). Or is it not, on the contrary, sometimes ambiguous? Mingled with suspicions and doubts? Mutilated? Adapted to our human points of view? To the criteria of fashion, feeling, human opinion?

Can we really make our own the words of Peter: "We must obey God rather than men"? (Acts 5:29)...

In the course of the centuries the "sanhedrins" that demand silence, the abandonment or distortion of this truth, change. The sanhedrins of the modern world are different—and they are numerous. These "sanhedrins" are individual men who reject divine truth; they are systems of human thought, of human knowledge; they are the different conceptions of the world and also the different programs of human behavior. They are also the various forms of pressure of so-called public opinion, of mass civilization, and of the media of social communications of a materialistic, lay, agnostic, and anti-religious hue. They are, finally, also some contemporary systems of government, which—if they do not deprive citizens completely of the possibility of confessing the faith—at least limit it in various ways, exclude believers, and make them second-class citizens....

Before all these modern forms of the Sanhedrin of [Peter's] time, the answer of faith always remains the same: "We must obey God rather than men. The God of our fathers raised Jesus, whom you killed by hanging him on a tree.... We are witnesses to these things, and so is the Holy Spirit" (see Acts 5:29-32). [OR 5-5-80, 8]

17. FAITH IS A TRUTH TO BE LIVED OUT

It is urgent to rediscover and set forth once more the authentic reality of the Christian faith, which is not simply a set of propositions to be accepted with intellectual assent. Rather, faith is a lived knowledge of Christ, a living remembrance of His commandments, and a *truth to be lived out*. A word, in any event, is not truly received until it passes into action, until it is put into practice. Faith is a decision involving one's whole existence. It is an encounter, a dialogue, a communion of love and of life between the believer and Jesus Christ, the Way, the Truth, and the Life (see John 14:6). It entails an act of trusting abandonment to Christ, which enables us to live as He lived (see Galatians 2:20), in profound love of God and of our brothers and sisters.

Faith also possesses a moral content. It gives rise to and calls for a consistent life commitment; it entails and brings to perfection the acceptance and observance of God's commandments. As St. John writes: "And by this we may be sure that we know Him, if we keep His commandments...." (1 Jn 2:3).

Through the moral life, faith becomes "confession," not only before God, but also before men; it becomes witness. "You are the light of the world," said Jesus. "Let your light so shine before men, that they may see your good works, and give glory to your Father who is in heaven" (Mt 5:14-16). [VS n. 88]

MARY, THE MODEL OF FAITH
The Mother of the Church is also the Mother of our faith, whose confident yes to the plan of God serves as our model of trust in Him.

THE WEEK OF MAY 4, 1997

18. MARY'S PLACE IN OUR JUBILEE PREPARATION

The Blessed Virgin... will be contemplated in this first year [of preparation, 1997] especially in the mystery of her Divine Motherhood. It was in her womb that the Word became flesh! The affirmation of the central place of Christ cannot therefore be separated from the recognition of the role played by His Most Holy Mother.

Veneration of her, when properly understood, can in no way take away from "the dignity and efficacy of Christ the one Mediator."[1] Mary in fact constantly points to her Divine Son and she is proposed to all believers as the model of faith which is put into practice. [TMA n. 43]

19. MARY'S "FIAT"

The mystery of the Incarnation was accomplished when Mary uttered her *fiat*—[that is,] "Let it be to me according to your word," which made possible, as far as it depended upon her in the divine plan, the granting of her Son's desire. Mary uttered this fiat in faith. In faith she entrusted herself to God without reserve and "devoted herself totally as the handmaid of the Lord to the person and work of her Son."[2] And—as the Fathers of the Church teach—she conceived this Son in her mind before she conceived Him in her womb: precisely in faith!

Rightly therefore does Elizabeth praise Mary: "And blessed is she who believed that there would be a fulfillment of what was spoken to her from the Lord" (Lk 1:45). [RMa n. 13]

20. MARY'S OBEDIENCE OF FAITH

Elizabeth's words [to Mary]: "And blessed is she who believed" do not apply only to that particular moment of the Annunciation. Certainly the Annunciation is the culminating moment of Mary's faith in her awaiting of Christ, but it is also the point of departure from which her whole journey toward God begins, her whole pilgrimage of faith. And on this road, in an eminent and truly heroic manner—indeed with an ever-greater heroism of faith—the obedience which she professes to the divine word of revelation will be fulfilled....

To believe means to abandon oneself to the truth of the word of the living God, knowing and humbly recognizing "how unsearchable are his judgments and how inscrutable his ways" (Rom 11:33). Mary, who by the eternal will of the Most High stands, one may say, at the very center of those "inscrutable ways" and "unsearchable judgments of God," conforms herself to them in the dim light of faith, accepting fully and with a ready heart everything that is decreed in the divine plan.... [RMa n. 14]

THE SACRAMENT OF BAPTISM

"As many of you as were baptized into Christ have put on Christ" (Gal 3:27). Baptism is our door into the life of Christ. As we meditate on Christ, then, we do well to meditate as well on the meaning of our Baptism.

THE WEEK OF MAY 25, 1997

21. THE VALUE OF BAPTISM

It is important to underscore the role and value of Baptism for entering the ecclesial community. Even today there are some who refuse to recognize this role, avoiding or delaying Baptism, particularly of children. According to the Church's established tradition, however, the Christian life does not simply begin with human dispositions, but with a sacrament endowed with divine efficacy.

Baptism as a sacrament, [that is,] as a visible sign of invisible grace, is the door through which God acts in the human soul—even in the soul of a newborn—to unite it to Himself in Christ and the Church. He makes it share in Redemption. He infuses new life into it. He makes it part of the communion of saints. He opens the way to the other sacraments, which serve to develop the Christian life fully. For this reason Baptism is like a rebirth by which a child of man becomes a child of God! [TPS 37/5, 1992, 238]

22. BORN AGAIN IN BAPTISM

Baptism regenerates us in the life of the Son of God; unites us to Christ and to His Body, the Church; anoints us in the Holy Spirit, making us spiritual temples.

We here recall Jesus' words to Nicodemus: "Truly, truly, I say to you, unless one is born of water and the Spirit, he cannot enter the kingdom of God" (Jn 3:5). Baptism, then, is a rebirth, a regeneration.

In considering this aspect of the gift which comes in Baptism, the Apostle Peter breaks out into song: "Blessed be the God and Father of our Lord Jesus Christ! By his great mercy we have been born anew to a living hope through the resurrection of Jesus Christ from the dead and to an inheritance which is imperishable, undefiled, and unfading" (1 Pt 1:3-4). And he calls Christians those who have been "born anew, not of perishable seed but of imperishable, through the living and abiding word of God" (1 Pt 1:23).

With Baptism we become children of God in his only-begotten Son, Jesus Christ. Rising from the waters of the baptismal font, every Christian hears again the voice that was once heard on the banks of the Jordan River: "You are my beloved Son; with you I am well pleased" (see Luke 3:22).

From this comes the understanding that one has been brought into association with the beloved Son, becoming a child of adoption (see Galatians 4:4-7) and a brother or sister of Christ. In this way the eternal plan of the Father for each person is realized in history: "For those whom he foreknew he also predestined to be conformed to the image of his Son, in order that he might be the first-born among many brethren" (Rom 8:29). [CL n. 10-11]

23. BAPTIZED INTO CHRIST'S BODY

Regenerated as children in the Son [of God], the baptized are inseparably joined together as "members of Christ and members of the body of the Church"[3].... Baptism symbolizes and brings about a mystical but real incorporation into the crucified and glorious Body of Christ. Through the sacrament Jesus unites the baptized to His death so as to unite the recipient to His Resurrection (see Romans 6:3-5). The "old man" is stripped away for reclothing with the "new man," that is, with Jesus Himself: "For as many of you as were baptized into Christ have put on Christ" (Gal 3:27; see also Ephesians 4:22-24; Colossians 3:9-10). The result is that "we, though many, are one body in Christ" (Rom 12:5).

In the words of St. Paul we find again the faithful echo of the teaching of Jesus Himself which reveals the mystical unity of Christ with His disciples and the disciples with each other. [He presents] it as an image and extension of that mystical communion that binds the Father to the Son and the Son to the Father in the bond of love, the Holy Spirit (see John

17:21). Jesus refers to this same unity in the image of the vine and the branches: "I am the vine, you are the branches" (Jn 15:5). [This] image... sheds light not only on the deep intimacy of the disciples with Jesus but on the necessity of a vital communion of the disciples with each other: all are branches of a single vine. [CL n. 12]

24. TEMPLES OF GOD'S SPIRIT

The Apostle Paul defines the baptized as "living stones" founded on Christ, the "cornerstone," and destined to "be raised up into a spiritual house" (see 1 Peter 2:5-8). The image introduces us to another aspect of the newness of Christian life coming from Baptism and described by the Second Vatican Council: "By regeneration and the anointing of the Holy Spirit, the baptized are consecrated into a spiritual house."[4]

The Holy Spirit "anoints" the baptized, sealing each with an indelible character (see 2 Corinthians 1:21-22), and constituting each as a spiritual temple. That is, He fills this temple with the holy presence of God as a result of each person's being united and likened to Jesus Christ.

With this spiritual "unction," Christians can repeat in an individual way the words of Jesus: "The Spirit of the Lord is upon me, because he has anointed me to preach the good news to the poor. He has sent me to proclaim release to captives and recovery of sight to the blind, to set at liberty those who are oppressed, to proclaim the acceptable year of the Lord" (see Luke 4:18-19; Isaiah 61:1-2). Thus with the outpouring of the Holy Spirit in Baptism and Confirmation, the baptized share in the same mission of Jesus as the Christ, the Savior-Messiah. [CL n. 13]

CATECHESIS

To dwell on Jesus Christ in our meditation is to unfold the riches of the Church's teaching about Him—to take part in the catechesis that is the lifeblood of faith.

THE WEEK OF JUNE 22, 1997

25. A PRIMARY TASK OF THE CHURCH

The Church has always considered catechesis one of her primary tasks, for, before Christ ascended to His Father after His Resurrection, He gave His Apostles a final command—to make disciples of all nations and to teach them to observe all that He had commanded (see Matthew 28:19-20). He thus entrusted them with the mission and power to proclaim to humanity what they had heard, what they had seen with their eyes, what they had looked upon and touched with their hands, concerning the Word of Life (see 1 John 1:1). He also entrusted them with the mission and power to explain with authority what He had taught them, His words and actions, His signs and commandments. And He gave them the Spirit to fulfill this mission.

Very soon the name of catechesis was given to the whole efforts within the Church to make disciples, to help people to believe that Jesus is the Son of God, so that believing, they might have life in His name (see John 20:31), and to educate and instruct them in this life and thus build up the Body of Christ. The Church has not ceased to devote her energy to this task. [CT n. 1]

26. CHRIST, THE HEART OF CATECHESIS

At the heart of catechesis we find, in essence, a Person, the Person of Jesus of Nazareth, "the only Son from the Father... full of grace and truth" (see John 1:14), who suffered and died for us, and who now, after rising, is living with us forever. It is Jesus who is "the way, and the truth, and the life" (Jn 14:6), and Christian living consists in following Christ....

The primary and essential object of catechesis is, to use an expression dear to St. Paul and also to contemporary theology, "the mystery of Christ." Catechizing is a way to lead a person to study this mystery in all its dimensions: "to make all men see what is the plan of the mystery,... comprehend with all the saints what is the breadth and length and height and depth,... know the love of Christ which surpasses knowledge,... [and be filled] with all the fullness of God" (Eph 3:9, 18-19).

[Catechesis] is therefore to reveal in the Person of Christ the whole of God's eternal design reaching fulfillment in that Person. It is to seek to understand the meaning of Christ's actions and words and of the signs worked by Him, for they simultaneously hide and reveal His mystery. Accordingly, the definitive aim of catechesis is to put people not only in touch but in communion, in intimacy, with Jesus Christ: only He can lead us to the love of the Father

44

in the Spirit and make us share in the life of the Holy Trinity. [CT n. 5]

27. THE AIM OF CATECHESIS

The specific aim of catechesis is to develop, with God's help, an as-yet initial faith, and to advance in fullness and to nourish day by day the Christian life of the faithful, young and old. It is in fact a matter of giving growth, at the level of knowledge and in life, to the seed of faith sown by the Holy Spirit with the initial proclamation and effectively transmitted by Baptism.

Catechesis aims therefore at developing understanding of the mystery of Christ in the light of God's word, so that the whole of a person's humanity is impregnated by that word. Changed by the working of grace into a new creature, the Christian thus sets himself to follow Christ and learns more and more within the Church to think like Him, to judge like Him, to act in conformity with His commandments, and to hope as He invites us to.

To put it more precisely: within the whole process of evangelization, the aim of catechesis is to be the teaching and maturation stage—that is to say, the period in which the Christian, having accepted by faith the person of Jesus Christ as the one Lord and having given Him complete adherence by sincere conversion of heart, endeavors to know better this Jesus to whom he has entrusted himself: to know His "mystery," the Kingdom of God proclaimed by Him, the requirements and promises contained in His Gospel message, and the paths that He has laid down for anyone who wishes to follow Him.

It is true that being a Christian means saying "yes" to Jesus Christ, but let us remember that this "yes" has two levels: it consists in surrendering to the Word of God and relying on it, but it also means, at a later stage, endeavoring to know better and better the profound meaning of this Word....

The one message—the Good News of salvation—that has been heard once or hundreds of times and has been accepted with the heart, is in catechesis probed unceasingly by reflection and systematic study, by awareness of its repercussions on one's personal life—an awareness calling for ever-greater commitment—and by inserting it into an organic and harmonious whole, namely, Christian living in society and the world.... The most valuable gift that the Church can offer to the bewildered and restless world of our time is to form within it Christians who are confirmed in what is essential and who are humbly joyful in their faith. [CT n. 20, 26, 61]

THE WEEK OF JULY 13, 1997

28. THE CATECHIST'S RESPONSIBILITY

Every catechist must constantly endeavor to transmit by his teaching and behavior the teaching and life of Jesus. He will not seek to keep directed toward himself and his personal opinions and attitudes the attention and the consent of the mind and heart of the person he is catechizing. Above all, he will not try to inculcate his personal opinions and options as if they expressed Christ's teaching and the lessons of His life. Every catechist should be able to apply to himself the mysterious words of Jesus: "My teaching is not mine, but his who sent me" (Jn 7:16).

St. Paul did this when he was dealing with a question of prime importance: "I received from the Lord what I also delivered to you" (1 Cor 11:23). What assiduous study of the word of God transmitted by the Church's Magisterium, what profound familiarity with Christ and with the Father, what a spirit of prayer, what detachment from self must a catechist have in order that he can say: "My teaching is not mine!" [CT n. 6]

29. The New Catechism

The [new] catechism of the Catholic Church... is a precious gift because it faithfully reiterates the Christian doctrine of all times. It is a rich gift due to the topics treated with care and depth. It is an opportune gift, given the demands and needs of the modern age.

Most of all, it is a true gift, a gift, that is, which presents the Truth revealed by God in Christ and entrusted by him to his Church....

This compendium of Catholic faith and morals is a privileged gift in which we have a convergence and collection in a harmonious synthesis of the Church's past, with her Tradition, her history of listening, proclaiming, celebrating, and witnessing to the Word, with her councils, doctors, and saints. Thus through successive generations resounds the enduring and ever-timely evangelical magisterium of Christ, light of mankind for twenty centuries....

[Yet] the catechism is also a gift looking to the future. From the meditative reflection on the mystery of Christ springs a courageous, generous teaching which the Church addresses to the future opening onto the third millennium. [TPS 38/3, 1993, 151-4]

VOCATION

The more deeply we come to know Christ, the more deeply we come to know ourselves, and we hear the voice of Christ calling us to that particular mission reserved for each us.

THE WEEK OF JULY 27, 1997

30. DISCOVERING OUR VOCATION

God calls me and sends me forth as a laborer in His vineyard. He calls me and sends me forth to work for the coming of His Kingdom in history. This personal vocation and mission defines the dignity and the responsibility of each member of the lay faithful. [It] makes up the focal point of the whole work of [spiritual] formation, whose purpose is the joyous and grateful recognition of this dignity and the faithful and generous living-out of this responsibility.

In fact, from eternity God has thought of us and has loved us as unique individuals. Every one of us He called by name, as the Good Shepherd "calls his sheep by name" (see John 10:3). However, only in the unfolding of the history of our lives and its events is the eternal plan of God revealed to each of us. Therefore, it is a gradual process; in a certain sense, one that happens day by day.

To be able to discover the actual will of the Lord in our lives always involves the following: a receptive listening to the Word of God and the Church, fervent and constant prayer, recourse to a wise and loving spiritual guide, and a faithful discernment of the gifts and talents given by God, as well as the diverse social and historical situations in which one lives.

Therefore, in the life of each member of the lay faithful there are particularly significant and decisive moments for discerning God's call and embracing the mission entrusted by Him. Among these are the periods of adolescence and young adulthood. No one must forget that the Lord, as the Master of the laborers in the vineyard, calls at every hour of life so as to make His holy will more precisely and explicitly known. Therefore, the fundamental and continuous attitude of the disciple should be one of vigilance and a conscious attentiveness to the voice of God.

It is not a question of simply *knowing* what God wants from each of us in the various situations of life. The individual must *do* what God wants, as we are reminded in the words that Mary, the Mother of Jesus, addressed to the servants at Cana: "Do whatever he tells you" (Jn 2:5).... This then is the marvelous yet demanding task awaiting all the lay faithful and all Christians at every moment: to grow always in the knowledge of the richness of Baptism and faith as well as to live it more fully. [CL n. 58]

31. THE CHURCH AND THE GIFT OF VOCATION

Each Christian vocation comes from God and is God's gift. However, it is never bestowed outside of or independently of the Church. Instead it always comes about in the Church because, as the Second Vatican Council reminds us, "God has willed to make men holy and save them, not as individuals without any bond or link between them, but rather to make them into a people who might acknowledge Him and serve Him in holiness...."[5] Christian vocation, whatever shape it takes, is a gift whose purpose is to build up the Church and to increase the Kingdom of God in the world. [PDV n. 35]

32. CALLED TO LIVE AN INTEGRATED LIFE

In discovering and living their proper vocation and mission, the lay faithful must be formed according to the union which exists from their being members of the Church and citizens of human society.

There cannot be two parallel lives in their existence: on the one hand, the so-called "spiritual" life, with its values and demands; and on the other, the so-called "secular" life, that is, life in a family, at work, in social relationships, in the responsibilities of public life and in culture. The branch, engrafted to the vine which is Christ, bears its fruit in every sphere of existence and activity. In fact, every area of the lay faithful's lives, as different as they are, enters into the plan of God who desires that these very areas be the places in time where the love of Christ is revealed and realized for both the glory of the Father and service of others.

Every activity, every situation, every precise responsibility—as, for example, skill and solidarity in work, love and dedication in the family and the education of children, service to society and public life, and the promotion of truth in the area of culture— [all these] are the occasions ordained by Providence

50

for a "continuous exercise of faith, hope and charity."[6] [CL n. 59]

SPIRITUAL DISCIPLINES

The life of Christ in us must be cultivated by the spiritual disciplines—habits of attitude and action that exercise and thus strengthen the virtues of faith, hope, and love.

THE WEEK OF AUGUST 17, 1997

33. DISCIPLINE AS AN IMITATION OF CHRIST

Life according to the Spirit, whose fruit is holiness (see Romans 6:22; Galatians 5:22), stirs up every baptized person and requires each to follow and imitate Jesus Christ. [We do this] in embracing the Beatitudes; in listening and meditating on the Word of God; in conscious and active participation in the liturgical and sacramental life of the Church; in personal prayer; in family or in community; in the hunger and thirst for justice; in the practice of the commandment of love in all circumstances of life and service to the brethren, especially the least, the poor and the suffering. [CL n. 16]

THE WEEK OF AUGUST 24, 1997

34. SCRIPTURE, THE WORD OF GOD

In order to recognize who Christ truly is, Christians, especially in the course of this [first] year [of preparation], should turn with renewed interest to the Bible, "whether it be through the liturgy, rich in the divine word, or through devotional reading, or through instructions suitable for the purpose and other aids."[7] In the revealed text it is the Heavenly Father Himself who comes to us in love and who dwells with us, disclosing to us the nature of His only-begotten Son and His plan of salvation for humanity. [TMA n. 40]

35. PRAYER, THE CENTER OF OUR LIVES

Truly Christian prayer... leads to sharing in the Son's own filial dialogue with the Father in accordance with St. Paul's marvelous expression in the Letter to the Galatians: "Because you are sons, God has sent the Spirit of his Son into our hearts, crying, 'Abba! Father!'" (Gal 4:6). Prayer is not one occupation among many, but is at the center of our life in Christ. It turns our attention away from ourselves and directs it to the Lord. Prayer fills the mind with truth and gives hope to the heart. Without a deep experience of prayer, growth in the moral life will be shallow. [TPS 39/2, 1994, 115-6]

36. PRAYER, AS ESSENTIAL AS BREATHING

"Lord, teach us to pray" (Lk 11:1). When, on the slopes of the Mount of Olives, the Apostles addressed Jesus with these words, they were not asking an ordinary question, but with spontaneous trust, they were expressing one of the deepest needs of the human heart.

To tell the truth, today's world does not make much room for that need. The hectic pace of daily activity, combined with the noisy and often frivolous invasiveness of the means of communication, is certainly not something conducive to the interior recollection required for prayer. Then, too, there are deeper difficulties: modern people have an increasingly less religious view of the world and life. The secularization process seems to have persuaded them that the course of events can be sufficiently explained by the interplay of this world's immanent forces, independent of higher intervention. The achievements of science and technology have also fostered their conviction that they already have, and will continue to increase, their ability to dominate situations, directing them according to their own desires.

In Christian circles, too, there is a widespread "functional" view of prayer which threatens to compromise its transcendent nature. Some claim that one truly finds God by being open to one's neighbor. Therefore, prayer would not mean being removed from the world's distractions in order to be recollected in conversation with God. It would rather be expressed in an unconditional commitment to charity for others. Authentic prayer, therefore, would be the works of charity, and they alone.

In reality, [however,] because they are creatures and of themselves incomplete and needy, human beings spontaneously turn to Him who is the source of every gift, in order to praise Him, make intercession, and in Him seek to fulfill the tormenting desire which enflames their hearts. St. Augustine understood this quite well when he noted: "You have made us for yourself, O Lord, and our hearts are restless until they rest in you...."

Christians know that for them prayer is as essential as breathing, and once they have tasted the sweetness of intimate conversation with God, they do not hesitate to immerse themselves in it with trusting abandonment. [TPS 38/1, 1993, 44-5]

37. A NECESSARY UNITY OF PRAYER AND ACTION

All of you, through the different forms of spirituality by which you are inspired and which constitute a rich spiritual heritage for the Church and humanity, are trying to live a really Christian and evangelical life, as laity and as Christians "in the world" without being "of the world" (Jn 17:11, 14). For you lay people, this apostolic life calls for effective openness to your various environments in order to cause the evangelical "leaven" to penetrate them. It involves multiple activities and responsibilities to be assumed in all areas of human life: the family, professions, society, culture, and politics. It is by assuming these responsibilities competently and in deep union with God that you will fulfill your vocation as laity and Christians: that you will sanctify yourselves and sanctify the world.

To remain united with God in the accomplishment of the tasks incumbent upon you is a vital necessity to bear witness to His love. Only a sacramental life and a life of prayer will be able to cause this intimacy with the Lord to grow.

To take time to pray, and to nourish prayer and activities through biblical, theological, and doctrinal study; to live by Christ and His grace by receiving assiduously the sacraments of reconciliation and the Eucharist—such are the fundamental requirements of every deeply Christian life. Thus the Holy Spirit will be the source both of your action and of your contemplation, which will then interpenetrate each other, support each other, and yield abundant fruit.

This deep unity between prayer and action is at the basis of all spiritual renewal, especially among the laity. It is at the basis of the great enterprises of evangelization and construction of the world according to God's plan. [OR 5-5-80, 5]

38. THE "CONTEMPLATIVE OUTLOOK"

We need... to foster, in ourselves and in others, a contemplative outlook. Such an outlook arises from faith in the God of life, who has created every individual as a wonder (see Psalms 139:14). It is the outlook of those who see life in its deeper meaning, who grasp its utter gratuitousness, its beauty, and its invitation to freedom and responsibility. It is the outlook of those who do not presume to take possession of reality but instead accept it as a gift, discovering in all things the reflection of the Creator and seeing in every person His living image (see Genesis 1:27; Psalms 8:5).

This outlook does not give into discouragement when confronted by those who are sick, suffering, outcast, or at death's door. Instead, in all these situations it feels challenged to find meaning, and precisely in the face of every person [it finds] a call to encounter, dialogue, and solidarity.

It is time for all of us to adopt this outlook, and with deep religious awe to rediscover the ability to revere and honor every person.... Inspired by this contemplative outlook, the new people of the redeemed cannot but respond with songs of joy, praise, and thanksgiving for the priceless gift of life, for the mystery of every individual's call to share through Christ in the life of grace and in an existence of unending communion with God our Creator and Father. [EV n. 83]

39. WHY SHOULD WE FAST?

Food and drink are indispensable for man to live. He uses them and must use them, but he may not abuse them in any way. The tradition of abstention from food and drink has as its purpose to introduce into man's existence not only the necessary balance, but also detachment from what might be defined [as] a "consumer attitude." In our times this attitude has become one of the characteristics of civilization and in particular of Western civilization.

The consumer attitude! Man geared to material goods, multiple material goods, very often misuses them. It is not a question here of just food and drink... Modern man must *fast,* that is, abstain not only from food and drink, but from many other means of consumption, stimulation, satisfaction of the senses....

Fasting is... more than mere abstinence from nourishment or material food; it represents a complex and deep reality. Fasting is a symbol, a sign, a serious and stimulating call to accept or to make renunciations. What renunciations? Renunciation of the "ego," that is, of so many caprices or unhealthy aspirations; renunciation of one's own defects, of impetuous passion, of unlawful desires. Fasting is being able to say no, bluntly and firmly, to what is suggested or asked by pride, selfishness, and vice; listening to one's own conscience; respecting the good of others; remaining faithful to God's holy law.

Fasting means putting a limit on so many desires, sometimes good ones, in order to have full mastery of oneself, to learn to control one's own instincts, to train the will in good. Acts of this kind were once known as "fioretti" (small acts of sacrifice). The name changes, but the substance remains! They were and remain acts of renunciation, carried out for love of the Lord or of Our Lady, with a noble purpose to attain. They were and are a "sport," an indispensable training in order to be victorious in the competitions of the spirit! Fasting, finally, means depriving oneself of something in order to meet the needs of one's brother, becoming in this way an exercise of goodness, of charity.

Fasting—understood, put into practice, lived in this way—becomes *repentance*, that is, *conversion to God*. For it purifies the heart from so much dross of evil, beautifies the soul with virtues, trains the will to good, dilates the heart to receive the abundance of divine grace. In this conversion, faith becomes stronger, hope more joyful, and charity more active! [OR 3-26-79, 1, 5]

THE WEEK OF OCTOBER 5, 1997

40. RESISTING TEMPTATION

The Lord Jesus Himself, the Son of God, "who in every respect has been tempted as we are, yet without sin" (see Hebrews 4:15), allowed Himself to be tempted by the evil one (see Matthew 4:1-11; Mark 1:12ff; Luke 4:1-13) in order to show that, like Himself, His followers too would be subjected to temptation, and in order to show how one should behave when subjected to temptation. For those who beseech the Father not to be tempted beyond their own strength (see 1 Corinthians 10:13) and not to succumb to temptation (see Matthew 6:13; Luke 11:4], and for those who do not expose themselves to occasions of sin, being subjected to temptation does not mean that they have sinned. Rather it is an opportunity for growing in fidelity and consistency through humility and watchfulness. [RP n. 26]

THE WEEK OF OCTOBER 12, 1997

41. WORK AS A SHARING IN GOD'S ACTIVITY

The Word of God's Revelation is profoundly marked by the fundamental truth that man, created in the image of God, shares by his work in the activity of the Creator; and that, within the limits of his own human capabilities, man in a sense continues to develop that activity, and perfects it as he advances further in the discovery of the resources and values contained in the whole of creation. We find this truth at the very beginning of Sacred Scripture, in the Book of Genesis, where the creation activity itself is presented in the form of "work" done by God during "six days," "resting" on the seventh day (see Genesis 2:2-3; Exodus 20:8, 11; Deuteronomy 5:12-14)....

Genesis... concludes the description of each day of creation with the statement: "And God saw that it was good" (see Genesis 1:4, 10, 12, 18, 21, 25, 31). This description of creation, which we find in the very first chapter of the Book of Genesis, is also in a sense the first "gospel of work." For it shows what the dignity of work consists of: it teaches that man ought to imitate God, his Creator, in working, because man alone has the unique characteristic of likeness to God. Man ought to imitate God both in working and also in resting, since God Himself wished to present His own creative activity under the form of work and rest. [LE n. 25]

42. CHRIST LOOKS WITH LOVE ON OUR WORK

The truth that by means of work man participates in the activity of God Himself, his Creator, was given particular prominence by Jesus Christ—the Jesus at whom many of His first listeners in Nazareth "were astonished, saying, 'Where did this man get all this? What is the wisdom given to him?... Is not this the carpenter?'" (Mk 6:2-3). For Jesus not only proclaimed, but first and foremost fulfilled by His deeds, the Gospel—the word of eternal Wisdom—that had been entrusted to Him. Therefore this was also "the gospel of work," because He who proclaimed it was Himself a man of work, a craftsman like Joseph of Nazareth (see Matthew 13:55)....

[Even] if we do not find in His words a special command to work—but rather on one occasion a prohibition against too much anxiety about work and life (see Matthew 6:25-34)—[nevertheless] at the same time the eloquence of the life of Christ is unequivocal: He belongs to the working world, He has appreciation and respect for human work. It can indeed be said that He looks with love upon human work and the different forms that it takes, seeing in each one of these forms a particular facet of man's likeness with God, the Creator and Father. [LE n. 25]

43. WORK IN THE LIGHT OF THE CROSS

All work, whether manual or intellectual, is inevitably linked with toil. The Book of Genesis expresses it in a truly penetrating manner: the original blessing of work contained in the very mystery of creation and connected with man's elevation as the image of God is contrasted with the curse that sin brought with it: "Cursed is the ground because of you; in toil you shall eat of it all the days of your life" (Gn 3:17)....

Sweat and toil, which work necessarily involves in the present condition of the human race, present the Christian and everyone who is called to follow Christ with the possibility of sharing lovingly in the work that Christ came to do. This work of salvation came about through suffering and death on a Cross. By enduring the toil of work in union with Christ crucified for us, man in a way collaborates with the Son of God for the redemption of humanity. He shows himself a true disciple of Christ by carrying the cross in his turn every day (see Luke 9:23) in the activity that he is called upon to perform.... The Christian finds in human work a small part of the Cross of Christ and accepts it in the same spirit of redemption in which Christ accepted his Cross for us. [LE n. 27]

44. GIVING ALMS

Alms, in itself, must be understood essentially as the attitude of a man who perceives the need of others, who wishes to share his own property with others.

Who will say that there will not always be another in need of help—spiritual [help], in the first place—support, comfort, brotherhood, and love? The world is always too poor in love.

Thus defined, to give alms is an act of very high positive value, the goodness of which must not be doubted, and which must find in us a fundamental readiness of heart and spirit, without which there is no real conversion to God.

Even if we do not have at our disposal riches and concrete capacities to meet the needs of our neighbor, we cannot feel dispensed from opening our heart to his necessities and relieving them as far as possible. Remember the widow's mite; she threw into the treasury of the temple only two small coins, but with them, all her great love: "for... she out of her poverty had put in all the living that she had" (see Luke 21:4)....

So it is, above all, the *interior value of the gift* that counts: the readiness to share everything, the readiness to give oneself. Let us here recall St. Paul: "If I give away all I have... but have not love, I gain nothing" (1 Cor 13:3). St. Augustine, too, writes well in this connection: "If you stretch out your hand to give, but have not mercy in your heart, you have not done anything; but if you have mercy in your heart, even when you have nothing to give with your hand, God accepts your alms."[8]

We are here touching the heart of the problem. In Holy Scripture and according to the evangelical categories, "alms" means in the first place an interior gift. *It means the attitude of opening to the other.* Precisely this attitude is an indispensable factor of *metanoia,* that is, conversion, just as prayer and fasting are also indispensable. [OR 4-2-79, 5, 12]

45. THE DISCIPLINE OF SIMPLICITY

In today's industrialized countries people are dominated by the frenzied race for possessing material goods. The consumer society makes the gap separating rich from poor even more obvious, and the uncontrolled search for a comfortable life risks blinding people to the needs of others. In order to promote the social, cultural, spiritual, and also economic welfare of all members of society, it is therefore absolutely essential to stem the unrestrained consumption of earthly goods and to control the creation of artificial needs.

Moderation and simplicity ought to become the criteria of our daily lives. The quantity of goods consumed by a tiny fraction of the world population produces a demand greater than available resources. A reduction of this demand constitutes a first step in alleviating poverty, provided that it is accompanied by effective measures to guarantee a fair distribution of the world's wealth.

In this regard, the Gospel invites believers not to accumulate the goods of this passing world: "Do not lay up for yourselves treasures on earth, where moth and rust consume and where thieves break in and steal, but lay up for yourselves treasures in heaven" (Mt 6:19-20). This is a duty intrinsic to the Christian vocation, no less than the duty of working to overcome poverty. And it is also a very effective means for succeeding in this task. [TPS 38/3, 1993, 159-160]

46. A RIGHT RELATION TO MATERIAL POSSESSIONS

A person who is concerned solely or primarily with possessing and enjoying, who is no longer able to control his instincts and passions, or to subordinate them by obedience to the truth, cannot be free. Obedience to the truth about God and humankind is the first condition of freedom, making it possible for a person to order his needs and desires and to choose the means of satisfying them according to a correct scale of values, so that the ownership of things may become an occasion of personal growth. [CA n. 41]

47. THE DISCIPLINE OF SUFFERING

The reality of suffering is ever before our eyes and often in the body, soul, and heart of each of us. Apart from faith, pain has always been a great riddle of human existence. Ever since Jesus, however, redeemed the world by His passion and death, a new perspective has been opened: through suffering one can grow in self-giving and attain the highest degree of love (see John 13:1), because of Him who "loved us and gave Himself up for us" (Eph 5:2). As a sharing in the mystery of the Cross, suffering can now be accepted and lived as a cooperation in Christ's saving mission....

In the Cross, the "Gospel of suffering" has been revealed to Christians. Jesus recognized in His sacrifice the way established by the Father for the redemption of humanity, and He followed this way.

He also told His disciples that they would be associated with this sacrifice: "I tell you truly, you will weep and mourn while the world rejoices" (see John 16:20).

This prediction, however, is not the only one, nor is it the final word, because it is completed by the announcement that their pain will be changed into joy: "You will grieve for a time, but your grief will be turned into joy" (see John 16:20). In the perspective of redemption, Christ's passion is oriented toward the Resurrection. Human beings too are thus associated with the mystery of the Cross in order to share joyfully in the mystery of the Resurrection.

For this reason Jesus did not hesitate to proclaim the blessedness of those who suffer: "Blest are the sorrowing; they shall be consoled.... Blest are those persecuted for holiness' sake; the reign of God is theirs. Blest are you when they insult you and persecute you and utter every kind of slander against you because of me. Be glad and rejoice, for your reward is great in heaven" (see Matthew 5:4, 10-12).

This blessedness can only be understood if one admits that human life is not limited to the time spent on earth, but is wholly directed to perfect joy and fullness of life in the hereafter. Earthly suffering, when accepted in love, is like a bitter kernel containing the seed of new life, the treasure of divine glory to be given man in eternity. Although the sight of a world burdened with evil and misfortune of every sort is often so wretched, nevertheless the hope of a better world of love and grace is hidden within it. It is hope that is nourished on Christ's promise.

With this support, those who suffer united in faith

with Him already experience in this life a joy that can seem humanly unexplainable. Heaven in fact begins on earth, beatitude is anticipated, so to speak, in the Beatitudes. "In holy people," St. Thomas Aquinas said, "there is a beginning of future happiness."[9] [TPS 39/5, 1994, 316-17]

48. THE FRUITFULNESS OF SUFFERING

[A] basic principle of the Christian faith is the fruitfulness of suffering and, hence, the call of all who suffer to unite themselves with Christ's redemptive sacrifice. Suffering thus becomes an offering, an oblation: this has happened and still does in so many holy souls.

Especially those who are oppressed by apparently senseless moral suffering find in Jesus' moral suffering the meaning of their own trials, and they go with Him into Gethsemane. In Him they find the strength to accept pain with holy abandon and trusting obedience to the Father's will. And they feel rising from within their hearts the prayer of Gethsemane: "But let it be as you would have it, Father, not as I" (see Mark 14:36). They mystically identify with Jesus when he was arrested: "Am I not to drink the cup the Father has given me?" (see John 18:11).

In Christ they also find the courage to offer their pain for the salvation of all, having learned the mysterious fruitfulness of every sacrifice from the offering on Calvary, according to the principle set forth by Jesus: "I solemnly assure you, unless the grain of wheat falls to the earth and dies, it remains just a grain of wheat. But if it dies, it produces much fruit" (see John 12:24).

Jesus' teaching is confirmed by the Apostle Paul, who had a very vivid awareness of sharing in Christ's passion in his own life and of the cooperation he could thus offer for the good of the Christian community. Because of union with Christ in suffering, he could speak of completing within himself what was lacking in the sufferings of Christ for the sake of His Body, the Church (see Colossians 1:24). Convinced of the fruitfulness of his union with the redeeming Passion, he stated: "Death is at work in us, but life in you" (2 Cor 4:12)...

Whoever follows Christ, whoever accepts St. Paul's theology of pain, knows that a precious grace, a divine favor, is connected with suffering, even if it is a grace that remains a mystery to us, because it is hidden under the appearances of a painful destiny. It is certainly not easy to discover in suffering the genuine divine love that wishes, through the acceptance of suffering, to raise human life to the level of Christ's saving love. Faith, however, enables us to cling to this mystery and, despite everything, brings peace and joy to the soul of the one suffering: at times he even says with St. Paul: "I am filled with consolation, and despite my many afflictions my joy knows no bounds" (see 2 Corinthians 7:4). [TPS 39/5, 1994, 317-18]

THE WEEK OF DECEMBER 7, 1997

49. HELPING OTHERS WHO SUFFER

Whoever relives the spirit of Christ's sacrifice is... moved to imitate Him by helping others who are suffering. Jesus relieved the countless human sufferings round about Him. In this respect too He is a perfect model. And He prescribed the command of mutual love that implies compassion and reciprocal aid.

In the parable of the Good Samaritan, Jesus teaches generous initiative on behalf of the suffering! He revealed His presence in all who are in need and pain, so that every act of helping the poor is done to Christ Himself….: "I assure you, as often as you did it for one of my least brothers, [he said,] you did it for me" (see Matthew 25:40). This means that suffering, intended to sanctify those who suffer, is also meant to sanctify those who help and comfort them. [TPS 39/5, 1994, 318]

ECUMENISM

As we turn toward Christ, we should also turn toward all those who call Him Lord and Savior, seeking that unity among Christians for which Christ Himself prayed to the Father.

THE WEEK OF DECEMBER 14, 1997

50. THE QUEST FOR CHRISTIAN UNITY

How can we fail to emphasize… the urgency of the quest for Christian unity? In order to face the missionary task which Providence today entrusts to us, it is essential that our apostolic commitment should proceed from a single faith proclaimed by hearts that are reconciled.

The saving message of which we are heralds will be accepted by the people of our time only if it is accompanied by a consistent witness. The Second Vatican Council states that "there can be no ecumenism worthy of the name without a change of heart. For it is from the renewal of our minds, from self-denial and an unstinted love, that desires of unity take their rise and develop."[10] In the light of that principle, it is fitting that we should examine ourselves concerning the direction which dialogue must take in accordance with the demands of the Gospel.

These are the demands of truth and love. They presuppose a frank recognition of the facts, together with a readiness to forgive and to make amends for our respective mistakes. They prevent us from shutting ourselves up within preconceptions, so often a source of bitterness and fruitless recriminations. They prevent us from making groundless accusations against our brother, imputing to him intentions and aims which he does not have. Thus, when we are impelled by a desire to understand fully the other's position, disagreements are settled through patient and sincere dialogue, under the guidance of the Holy Spirit....

The Catholic Church intends to seek this unity, and to continue unfailingly her commitment to ecumenism. With the help of God, she will not yield in the face of difficulties and failures. She is aware of her obligation to respond to the invitation "that they may all be one" (Jn 17:21), bequeathed by Jesus to believers as His final charge before His death on the Cross.... How urgent it is to unite the efforts of all the churches and Christian communities for a new and courageous evangelization! [TPS 37/3, 1992, 147-8]

51. ECUMENICAL RECONCILIATION

To the people of our time, so sensitive to the proof of concrete living witness, the Church is called upon to give an example of reconciliation particularly within herself. And for this purpose we must all work to bring peace to people's minds, to reduce tensions, to overcome divisions, and to heal wounds that may have been inflicted by brother on brother.... We must try to be united in what is essential for Christian faith and life, in accordance with the ancient maxim: In what is doubtful, freedom; in what is necessary, unity; in all things, charity.

It is in accordance with this same criterion that the Church must conduct her ecumenical activity. For in order to be completely reconciled, she knows that she must continue the quest for unity among those who are proud to call themselves Christians but who are separated from one another, also as churches or communions, and from the Church of Rome.

The latter seeks a unity which, if it is to be the fruit and expression of true reconciliation, is meant to be based neither upon a disguising of the points that divide nor upon compromises which are as easy as they are superficial and fragile. Unity must be the result of a true conversion of everyone, the result of mutual forgiveness, of theological dialogue and fraternal relations, of prayer, and of complete docility to the action of the Holy Spirit, who is also the Spirit of Reconciliation. [RP n. 9]

52. CHRIST, THE ECUMENICAL CENTER

All of us who are Christ's followers must... meet and unite around Him. This unity in the various fields of the life, tradition, structures, and discipline of the individual Christian churches and ecclesial communities cannot be brought about without effective work aimed at getting to know each other and removing the obstacles blocking the way to perfect unity. However, we can and must immediately reach and display to the world our unity in proclaiming the mystery of Christ, in revealing the divine dimension and also the human dimension of the Redemption, and in struggling with unwearying perseverance for the dignity that each human being has reached and can continually reach in Christ....

Jesus Christ is the stable principle and fixed center of the mission that God Himself has entrusted to man. We must all share in this mission and concentrate all our forces on it, since it is more necessary than ever for modern mankind. [RH n. 11]

1998

YEAR TWO OF PREPARATION:
Focusing on God the Holy Spirit

The Holy Spirit of God

We turn from our reflections in the first year on God the Son in order to ponder in the second year the mystery of God the Holy Spirit, "the uncreated Gift" sent by the Son to fill the Church with His power.

THE WEEK OF JANUARY 4, 1998

1. The Spirit of Holiness

[Jesus says,] "The Spirit of the Lord is upon me" (Lk 4:18). The Spirit is not simply upon the Messiah, but He fills Him, penetrating every part of Him and reaching to the very depths of all that He is and does. Indeed, the Spirit is the principle of the consecration and mission of the Messiah: "Because he has anointed me and sent me to preach good news to the poor" (see Luke 4:18). Through the Spirit, Jesus belongs totally and exclusively to God and shares in the infinite holiness of God, who calls Him, chooses Him, and sends Him forth. In this way the Spirit of the Lord is revealed as the source of holiness and of the call of holiness.

This same "Spirit of the Lord" is upon the entire people of God, which becomes established as a people consecrated to God and sent by God to announce the Gospel of salvation. The members of the People of God are "inebriated" and "sealed" with the Spirit (see 1 Corinthians 12:13; 2 Corinthians 1:21ff; Ephesians 1:13; 4:30) and called to holiness.

In particular, the Spirit reveals to us and communicates the fundamental calling which the Father addresses to everyone from all eternity: the vocation to be "holy and blameless before him...in love," by virtue of our predestination to be His adopted

73

children through Jesus Christ (Eph 1:4-5). This is not all. By revealing and communicating this vocation to us, the Spirit becomes within us the principle and wellspring of its fulfillment. He, the Spirit of the Son (see Galatians 4:6), configures us to Christ Jesus and makes us sharers in His life as Son—that is, sharers in His life of love for the Father and for our brothers and sisters.

"If we live by the Spirit, let us also walk by the Spirit" (Gal 5:25). In these words the Apostle Paul reminds us that a Christian life is a spiritual life, that is, a life enlivened and led by the Spirit toward holiness or the perfection of charity. [PDV n. 19]

2. THE HOLY SPIRIT, UNCREATED GIFT

The Holy Spirit does not cease to be the guardian of hope in the human heart: the hope of all human creatures, and especially of those who "have the first fruits of the Spirit" and "wait for the redemption of their bodies" (see Romans 8:23).

The Holy Spirit, in His mysterious bond of divine communion with the Redeemer of man, is the One who brings about the continuity of His work. He takes from Christ and transmits to all, unceasingly entering into the history of the world through the heart of man. Here He becomes—as the liturgical Sequence of the Solemnity of Pentecost proclaims—the true "father of the poor, giver of gifts, light of hearts."

He becomes the "sweet guest of the soul," whom the Church unceasingly greets on the threshold of the inmost sanctuary of every human being. For He brings rest and relief in the midst of toil, in the midst of the work of human hands and minds. He brings rest and ease in the midst of the heat of the day, in the midst of the anxieties, struggles, and perils of every age. He brings consolation, when the human heart grieves and is tempted to despair.

And therefore the same Sequence exclaims: "without your aid nothing is in man, nothing is without fault." For only the Holy Spirit "convinces concerning sin" (see John 16:8), concerning evil, in order to restore what is good in man and in the world: in order to "renew the face of the earth" (Ps 104:30). Therefore, He purifies from everything that disfigures man, from what is unclean. He heals even the deepest wounds of human existence. He changes the interior dryness of souls, transforming them into the fertile fields of grace and holiness. What is hard He softens, what is frozen He warms, what is wayward He sets anew on the paths of salvation.

Praying thus, the Church unceasingly professes her faith that there exists in our created world a Spirit who is an uncreated gift. He is the Spirit of the Father and of the Son: like the Father and the Son He is uncreated, without limit, eternal, omnipotent, God, Lord. This Spirit of God fills the universe, and all that is created recognizes in Him the source of its own identity, finds in Him its own transcendent expression, turns to Him and awaits Him, invokes Him with its own being. Man turns to Him,... the Spirit of truth and of love, man who lives by truth and by love, and who without the source of truth and love cannot live. [DV n. 67]

3. THE HOLY SPIRIT, HELP OF THE CHURCH

To [the Holy Spirit] turns the Church, which is the heart of humanity, to implore for all and dispense to all those gifts of the love which through Him "has been poured into our hearts" (Rom 5:5). To Him turns the Church, along the intricate paths of man's pilgrimage on earth: she implores, she unceasingly implores uprightness of human acts, as the Spirit's work. She implores the joy and consolation that only He, the true Counselor, can bring by coming down into people's inmost hearts. The Church implores the grace of the virtues that merit heavenly glory, implores eternal salvation, in the full communication of the divine life, to which the Father has eternally "predestined" human beings, created through love in the image and likeness of the Most Holy Trinity.

The Church with her heart which embraces all human hearts implores from the Holy Spirit that happiness which only in God has its complete realization: the joy that no one will be able to take away (see John 16:22), the joy which is the fruit of love, and therefore of God who is love. She implores "the righteousness, the peace, and the joy of the Holy Spirit" in which, in the words of St. Paul, consists the Kingdom of God (see Romans 14:17, Galatians 5:22). [DV n. 67]

4. THE FRUIT OF THE SPIRIT

The history of salvation shows that God's coming close and making Himself present to man and the world—that marvelous "condescension" of the Spirit—meets with resistance and opposition in our human reality.... It is St. Paul who describes in a particularly eloquent way the tension and struggle that trouble the human heart. We read in the Letter to the Galatians: "But I say, walk by the Spirit, and do not gratify the desires of the flesh. For the desires of the flesh are against the Spirit, and the desires of the Spirit are against the flesh; for these are opposed to each other, to prevent you from doing what you would" (Gal 5:16-17).

There already exists in man, as a being made up of body and spirit, a certain tension, a certain struggle of tendencies between the "spirit" and the "flesh." But this struggle in fact belongs to the heritage of sin, is a consequence of sin and at the same time a confirmation of it. This is part of everyday experience. As the Apostle writes: "Now the works of the flesh are plain: fornication, impurity, licentiousness... drunkenness, carousing and the like." These are the sins that could be called "carnal." But he also adds others: "enmity, strife, jealousy, anger, selfishness, dissension, party spirit, envy" (see Galatians 5:19-21). All of this constitutes the "works of the flesh."

But with these works, which are undoubtedly evil, Paul contrasts "the fruit of the Spirit," such as "love, joy, peace, patience, kindness, goodness, faithfulness, gentleness, self-control" (Gal 5:22-23). From the context it is clear that for the Apostle it is not a question of discriminating against and condemning the body, with which the spiritual soul constitutes man's nature.... Rather, he is concerned with the morally good or bad works, or better, the permanent dispositions—virtues and vices—which are the fruit of submission to (in the first case) or of resistance to (in the second case) the saving action of the Holy Spirit. Consequently the Apostle writes: "If we live by the Spirit, let us also walk by the Spirit" (Gal 5:25)....

The contrast that St. Paul makes between life "according to the Spirit" and life "according to the flesh" (see Romans 8:5, 9) gives rise to a further contrast: that between life and death. "To set the mind on the flesh is death, but to set the mind on the Spirit is life and peace"; hence the warning: "For if you live according to the flesh you will die, but if by the Spirit you put to death the deeds of the body you will live" (Rom 8:6, 13, RSV). Properly understood, this is an exhortation to live in the truth, that is, according to the dictates of an upright conscience, and at the same time it is a profession of faith in the Spirit of truth as the One who gives life. [DV n. 55]

THE WEEK OF FEBRUARY 1, 1998

5. THE HOLY SPIRIT AND PRAYER

The breath of the divine life, the Holy Spirit, in its simplest and most common manner, expresses itself and makes itself felt in prayer. It is a beautiful and salutary thought that, wherever people are praying in the world, there the Holy Spirit is, the living breath of prayer. It is a beautiful and salutary thought to recognize that—if prayer is offered throughout the world, in the past, in the present, and in the future—equally widespread is the presence and action of the Holy Spirit, who "breathes" prayer in the heart of man in all the endless range of the most varied situations and conditions, sometimes favorable and sometimes unfavorable to the spiritual and religious life.

Many times, through the influence of the Spirit, prayer rises from the human heart in spite of prohibitions and persecutions and even official proclamations regarding the nonreligious or even atheistic character of public life. Prayer always remains the voice of all those who apparently have no voice—and in this voice there always echoes that "loud cry" attributed to Christ by the Letter to the Hebrews (see Hebrews 5:7).

Prayer is also the revelation of that abyss which is the heart of man: a depth which comes from God and which only God can fill, precisely with the Holy Spirit. We read in Luke: "If you, then, who are evil, know how to give good gifts to your children, how much more will the heavenly Father give the Holy Spirit to those who ask him" (Lk 11:13).

The Holy Spirit is the gift that comes into man's heart together with prayer. In prayer He manifests Himself first of all and above all as the gift that "helps us in our weakness" (Rom 8:26). This is the magnificent thought developed by St. Paul in the Letter to the Romans, when he writes: "For we do not know how to pray as we ought, but the Spirit himself intercedes for us with sighs too deep for words" (Rom 8:26).

Therefore, the Holy Spirit not only enables us to pray, but guides us from within in prayer: He is present in our prayer and gives it a divine dimension. Thus "he who searches the hearts of men knows what is the mind of the Spirit, because the Spirit intercedes for the saints according to the will of God" (Rom 8:27). Prayer through the power of the Holy Spirit becomes the evermore mature expression of the new man, who by means of this prayer participates in the divine life. [DV n. 65]

6. "RECEIVE THE HOLY SPIRIT!"

The whole person, body and soul, is destined to eternal life. And eternal life is life in God. Not life in the world, which, as St. Paul teaches, is "subjected to futility" (Rom 8:20). As a creature in the world, the individual is subject to death, just like every other created being. The immortality of the whole person can come only as a gift from God. It is in fact a sharing in the eternity of God Himself.

How do we receive this life in God? Through the Holy Spirit! Only the Holy Spirit can give this new life, as we profess in the Creed: "I believe in the Holy Spirit, the Lord, the giver of life." Through Him we become, in the likeness of the only-begotten Son, adopted children of the Father.

When Jesus says, "Receive the Holy Spirit!" (Jn 20:22) He is saying: Receive from Me this divine life, the divine adoption which I brought into the world and which I grafted on to human history. I myself, the Eternal Son of God, through the power of the Holy Spirit, became the Son of Man, born of the Virgin Mary. You, through the power of the same Spirit, must become—in Me and through Me— adopted sons and daughters of God.

"Receive the Holy Spirit!" means: Accept from Me

this inheritance of grace and truth, which makes you one spiritual and mystical body with Me. "Receive the Holy Spirit!" also means: Become sharers in the Kingdom of God, which the Holy Spirit pours into your hearts as the fruit of the suffering and sacrifice of the Son of God, so that more and more God will become all in all (see 1 Corinthians 15:28). [TPS 40/3, 1995, 164-5]

THE VIRTUE OF HOPE

It is "by the power of the Holy Spirit," the Apostle Paul says, that we are able to "abound in hope." His comforting presence today encourages us to place our tomorrow in the hands of "the God of hope" who loves us (Rom 15:13).

THE WEEK OF FEBRUARY 15, 1998

7. HOPE FOR THE THIRD MILLENNIUM

Believers should be called to a renewed appreciation of the theological virtue of hope, which they have already heard proclaimed "in the word of the truth, the Gospel" (Col 1:5). The basic attitude of hope, on the one hand, encourages the Christian not to lose sight of the final goal which gives meaning and value to life; and on the other, [it] offers solid and profound reasons for a daily commitment to God's plan.

As the Apostle Paul reminds us: "We know that the whole creation has been groaning in travail together until now; and not only the creation, but we ourselves, who have the first fruits of the Spirit, groan inwardly as we wait for adoption as sons, the redemption of our bodies. For in this hope we were saved"

(Rom 8:22-24). Christians are called to prepare for the Great Jubilee of the beginning of the third millennium by renewing their hope in the definitive coming of the Kingdom of God, preparing for it daily in their hearts, in the Christian community to which they belong, in their particular social context, and in world history itself. [TMA n. 46]

8. SIGNS OF HOPE

There is... a need for a better appreciation and understanding of the signs of hope present in the last part of this century, even though they often remain hidden from our eyes. In society in general, such signs of hope include scientific, technological, and especially medical progress in the service of human life; a greater awareness of our responsibility for the environment; efforts to restore peace and justice wherever they have been violated; a desire for reconciliation and solidarity among different peoples, particularly in the complex relationship between the north and the south of the world.

In the Church, [signs of hope] include a greater attention to the voice of the Spirit through the acceptance of charisms and the promotion of the laity; a deeper commitment to the cause of Christian unity; and the increased interest in dialogue with other religions and with contemporary culture. [TMA n. 46]

9. THE HOLY SPIRIT, GUARDIAN OF HOPE

The Church, united with the Virgin Mother, prays unceasingly as the Bride to her divine Spouse, as the words of the Book of Revelation.... attest: "The Spirit and the bride say to the Lord Jesus Christ: Come!" (see Revelation 22:17). The Church's prayer is this unceasing invocation, in which "the Spirit himself intercedes for us" (Rom 8:26). In a certain sense, the Spirit Himself utters it *with* the Church and *in* the Church.

For the Spirit is given to the Church in order that through His power the whole community of the People of God, however widely scattered and diverse, may persevere in hope: that hope in which "we have been saved" (see Romans 8:24). It is... the hope of definitive fulfillment in God, the hope of the eternal Kingdom, that is brought about by participation in the life of the Trinity. The Holy Spirit, given to the Apostles as the Counselor, is the guardian and animator of this hope in the heart of the Church. [DV n. 66]

10. SPIRITUAL HUNGER IS A SIGN OF HOPE

Our times are both momentous and fascinating. While on the one hand people seem to be pursuing material prosperity and to be sinking ever deeper into consumerism and materialism, on the other hand we are witnessing a desperate search for meaning, the need for an inner life, and a desire to learn new forms and methods of meditation and prayer. Not only in cultures with strong religious elements,

83

but also in secularized societies, the spiritual dimension of life is being sought after as an antidote to dehumanization.

This phenomenon—the so-called "religious revival"—is not without ambiguity, but it also represents an opportunity. The Church has an immense spiritual patrimony to offer humankind, a heritage in Christ, who called Himself "the way, and the truth, and the life" (Jn 14:6): It is the Christian path to meeting God, to prayer, to asceticism, and to the search for life's meaning. [RM n. 38]

11. RENEWAL OF PRAYER IS A SIGN OF HOPE

Our difficult age has a special need of prayer. In the course of history—both in the past and in the present—many men and women have borne witness to the importance of prayer by consecrating themselves to the praise of God and to the life of prayer, especially in monasteries and convents. So, too, recent years have been seeing a growth in the number of people who, in evermore widespread movements and groups, are giving first place to prayer and seeking in prayer a renewal of their spiritual life. This is a significant and comforting sign, for from this experience there is coming a real contribution to the revival of prayer among the faithful, who have been helped to gain a clearer idea of the Holy Spirit as He who inspires in hearts a profound yearning for holiness.

In many individuals and many communities there is a growing awareness that, even with all the rapid progress of technological and scientific civilization, and despite the real conquests and goals attained, man is threatened, humanity is threatened. In the face of this danger, and indeed already experiencing the frightful reality of man's spiritual decadence, individuals and whole communities, guided as it were by an inner sense of faith, are seeking the strength to raise man up again, to save him from himself, from his own errors and mistakes that often make harmful his very conquests. And thus they are discovering prayer, in which the "Spirit who helps us in our weakness" manifests Himself. In this way the times in which we are living are bringing the Holy Spirit closer to the many who are returning to prayer. [DV n. 65]

THE WEEK OF MARCH 22, 1998

12. A NEW SPRINGTIME FOR THE GOSPEL

If we look at today's world, we are struck by many negative factors that can lead to pessimism. But this feeling is unjustified: we have faith in God our Father and Lord, in His goodness and mercy. As the third millennium of the Redemption draws near, God is preparing a great springtime for Christianity, and we can already see its first signs. In fact, both in the non-Christian world and in the traditionally Christian world, people are gradually drawing closer to Gospel ideals and values, a development which the Church seeks to encourage. Today in fact there is a new consensus among peoples about these values: the rejection of violence and war; respect for the human person and for human rights; the desire for freedom, justice, and brotherhood; the surmounting of different forms of racism and nationalism; the affirmation of the dignity and role of women.

Christian hope sustains us in committing ourselves fully to the new evangelization and to the
worldwide mission, and leads us to pray as Jesus
taught us: "Thy kingdom come. Thy will be done, on
earth as it is in heaven" (Mt 6:10).

MARY, MODEL OF HOPE
*Our Lord's Mother lived her life in the firm hope that God's
promises to her would be fulfilled; she has become for us the
Mother of hope.*

THE WEEK OF MARCH 29, 1998
13. MARY, WOMAN OF HOPE
Mary, who conceived the Incarnate Word by the
power of the Holy Spirit—and then in the whole of
her life allowed herself to be guided by His interior
activity—will be contemplated and imitated during
this year above all as the woman who was docile to
the voice of the Spirit, a woman of silence and attentiveness, a woman of hope who, like Abraham,
accepted God's will "hoping against hope" (see
Romans 4:18). Mary gave full expression to the longing of the poor of Yahweh and is a radiant model for
those who entrust themselves with all their hearts to
the promises of God. [TMA n. 48]

THE WEEK OF APRIL 5, 1998
14. MARY, HOPE IN OUR STRUGGLE WITH SIN
In the [saving] design of the Most Holy Trinity, the
mystery of the Incarnation constitutes the super-
abundant fulfillment of the promise made by God to

man after original sin, after that first sin whose effects oppress the whole earthly history of man (see Genesis 3:15). And so, there comes into the world a Son, "the seed of the woman" who will crush the evil of sin in its very origins: "he will crush the head of the serpent."...The victory of the woman's Son will not take place without a hard struggle, a struggle that is to extend through the whole of human history....

Mary, Mother of the Incarnate Word, is placed at the very center of that... struggle which accompanies the history of humanity on earth and the history of salvation itself. In this central place, she who belongs to the weak and poor of the Lord (see Luke 1:46-55) bears in herself, like no other member of the human race, that glory of grace which the Father has bestowed on us in His Beloved Son, and this grace determines the extraordinary greatness and beauty of her whole being. Mary thus remains before God, and also before the whole of humanity, as the unchangeable and inviolable sign of God's election, spoken of in Paul's letter: "in Christ... he chose us... before the foundation of the world... he destined us... to be his sons" (Eph 1:4-5].

This election is more powerful than any experience of evil and sin... which marks the history of man. In this history Mary remains a sure sign of hope. [RMa n. 11]

THE WEEK OF APRIL 12, 1998

15. MARY, SIGN OF SURE HOPE

The angel's Annunciation to Mary is framed by these reassuring words: "Do not be afraid, Mary," and, "With God nothing will be impossible" (Lk 1:30, 37.

The whole of the Virgin Mother's life is in fact pervaded by the certainty that God is near to her and that He accompanies her with His providential care.

The same is true of the Church, which finds "a place prepared by God" (Rv 12:6) in the desert, the place of trial but also of the manifestation of God's love for his people (see Hosea 2:16). Mary is a living word of comfort for the Church in her struggle against death. Showing us the Son, the Church assures us that in Him the forces of death have already been defeated: "Death with life contended: combat strangely ended! Life's own Champion, slain, yet lives to reign."[1]

The Lamb who was slain is alive, bearing the marks of His Passion in the splendor of the Resurrection. He alone is master of all the events of history: He opens its "seals" (see Revelation 5:1-10) and proclaims, in time and beyond, the power of life over death. In the new Jerusalem, that new world toward which human history is traveling, "death shall be no more, neither shall there be mourning nor crying nor pain any more, for the former things have passed away" (Rv 21:4, RSV).

And as we, the pilgrim people, the people of life and for life, make our way in confidence toward a "new heaven and a new earth" (Rv 21:1), we look to her who is for us "a sign of sure hope and solace."[2] [EV n. 105]

THE CHURCH

The Church was born on the day of Pentecost, when the Spirit came upon Christ's followers; the Spirit is the One who empowers the Church to be a sacrament of Christ's life in the world.

THE WEEK OF APRIL 19, 1998

16. CHRIST COMES TO THE CHURCH THROUGH THE HOLY SPIRIT

As the end of the second Millennium approaches— an event which should recall to everyone and as it were make present anew the coming of the Word [that is, Christ] in the fullness of time—the Church once more means to ponder the very essence of her divine-human constitution and of that mission which enables her to share in the messianic mission of Christ.... Following this line, we can go back to the Upper Room, where Jesus Christ reveals the Holy Spirit as the Paraclete [Advocate], the Spirit of truth, and where He speaks of His own departure through the Cross as the necessary condition for the Spirit's coming: "It is to your advantage that I go away, for if I do not go away, the Counselor will not come to you; but if I go, I will send him to you" (Jn 16:7).... This prediction first came true the evening of Easter day and then during the celebration of Pentecost in Jerusalem, and... ever since then it is being fulfilled in human history through the Church.

In the light of that prediction, we also grasp the full meaning of what Jesus says, also at the Last

Supper, about His new coming. For it is significant that in the same farewell discourse Jesus foretells not only His departure but also His new coming. His exact words are: "I will not leave you desolate; I will come to you" (Jn 14:18). And at the moment of His final farewell before He ascends into heaven, He will repeat even more explicitly: "Lo, I am with you," and this [will be] "always, to the close of the age" (Mt 28:20).

This new coming of Christ, this continuous coming of His, in order to be with His Apostles, with the Church... occurs by the power of the Holy Spirit, who makes it possible for Christ, who has gone away, to come now and for ever in a new way. This new coming of Christ by the power of the Holy Spirit, and His constant presence and action in the spiritual life, are accomplished in the sacramental reality. In this reality, Christ, who has gone away in His visible humanity, comes, is present, and acts in the Church in such an intimate way as to make it His own Body. As such, the Church lives, works, and grows "to the close of the age." All this happens through the power of the Holy Spirit. [DV n. 61]

THE WEEK OF APRIL 26, 1998

17. THE CHURCH, GREAT SACRAMENT OF RECONCILIATION

According to our faith, the Word of God became flesh and came to dwell in the world.... By conquering through His death on the Cross evil and the power of sin, by His loving obedience, He brought salvation to all and became reconciliation for all. In Him God reconciled man to Himself....

The Church has the mission of proclaiming this reconciliation and as it were of being its sacrament in the world. The Church is the sacrament, that is to say, the sign and means of reconciliation, in different ways which differ in value but which all come together to obtain what the divine initiative of mercy desires to grant to humanity.

She is a sacrament in the first place by her very existence as a reconciled community which witnesses to and represents in the world the work of Christ.

She is also a sacrament through her service as the custodian and interpreter of sacred Scripture, which is the Good News of reconciliation inasmuch as it tells each succeeding generation about God's loving plan and shows to each generation the paths to universal reconciliation in Christ.

Finally, she is a sacrament by reason of the seven sacraments which, each in its own way, "make the Church."[3] For since they commemorate and renew Christ's Paschal Mystery, all the sacraments are a source of life for the Church, and in the Church's hands they are a means of conversion to God and of reconciliation among people. [RP n. 11]

THE WEEK OF MAY 3, 1998

18. THE CHURCH'S WORK OF RECONCILIATION

The mission of reconciliation is proper to the whole Church, also and especially to that Church which has already been admitted to the full sharing in divine glory with the Virgin Mary—the angels and the saints, who contemplate and adore the thrice-holy God. The Church in heaven, the Church on earth,

91

and the Church in purgatory are mysteriously united in this cooperation with Christ in reconciling the world to God.

The first means of this [saving] action is that of prayer. It is certain that the Blessed Virgin, Mother of Christ and of the Church, and the saints, who have now reached the end of their earthly journey and possess God's glory, sustain by their intercession their brethren who are on pilgrimage through the world, in the commitment to conversion, to faith, to getting up again after every fall, to acting in order to help the growth of communion and peace in the Church and in the world. In the mystery of the communion of saints, universal reconciliation is accomplished in its most profound form, which is also the most fruitful for the salvation of all.

There is yet another means: that of preaching. The Church, since she is the disciple of the one Teacher Jesus Christ, in her own turn as mother and teacher untiringly exhorts people to reconciliation. And she does not hesitate to condemn the evil of sin, to proclaim the need for conversion, to invite and ask people to let themselves be reconciled. In fact, this is her prophetic mission in today's world, just as it was in the world of yesterday. It is the same mission as that of her Teacher and Head, Jesus. Like Him, the Church will always carry out this mission with sentiments of merciful love and will bring to all people those words of forgiveness and that invitation to hope which come from the Cross.

There is also the often so difficult and demanding means of pastoral action aimed at bringing back every individual—whoever and wherever he or she may be—to the path, at times a long one, leading back to the Father in the communion of all the brethren.

Finally, there is the means of witness, which is almost always silent. This is born from a twofold awareness on the part of the Church: that of being in herself "unfailingly holy,"[4] but also the awareness of the need to go forward and "daily be further purified and renewed, against the day when Christ will present her to Himself in all her glory without spot or wrinkle"—for, by reason of her sins, sometimes "the radiance of the Church's face shines less brightly" in the eyes of those who behold her.[5]

This witness cannot fail to assume two fundamental aspects. This first aspect is that of being the sign of that universal charity which Jesus Christ left as an inheritance to His followers, as a proof of belonging to His Kingdom. The second aspect is [her] translation into ever-new manifestations of conversion and reconciliation both within the Church and outside her, by the overcoming of tensions, by mutual forgiveness, by growth in the spirit of brotherhood and peace which is to be spread throughout the world. By this means the Church will effectively be able to work for the creation of what my predecessor Paul VI called the "civilization of love." [RP n. 12]

19. THE CHURCH'S WITNESS TO MORAL TRUTH

The Church's teaching, and particularly her firmness in defending the universal and permanent validity of the precepts prohibiting intrinsically evil acts, is not infrequently seen as the sign of an intolerable intransigence, particularly with regard to the enormously complex and conflict-filled situations present in the moral life of individuals and of society today. This intransigence is said to be in contrast with the Church's motherhood. The Church, one hears, is lacking in understanding and compassion.

But the Church's motherhood can never in fact be separated from her teaching mission, which she must always carry out as the faithful Bride of Christ, who is the Truth in person. "As teacher, she never tires of proclaiming the moral norm.... The Church is in no way the author or the arbiter of this norm. In obedience to the truth which is Christ, whose image is reflected in the nature and dignity of the human person, the Church interprets the moral norm and proposes it to all people of good will, without concealing its demands of radicalness and perfection."[6]

In fact, genuine understanding and compassion must mean love for the person, for his true good, for his authentic freedom. And this does not result, certainly, from concealing or weakening moral truth, but rather from proposing it in its most profound meaning as an outpouring of God's eternal wisdom, which we have received in Christ, and as a service to man, to the growth of his freedom and to the attainment of his happiness. Still, a clear and forceful presentation of moral truth can never be separated from a profound and heartfelt respect, born of that patient and trusting love which man always needs along his moral journey, a journey frequently wearisome on account of difficulties, weakness, and painful situations. [VS n. 95]

20. THE MEANING OF THE KINGDOM OF GOD

Nowadays the Kingdom [of God] is much spoken of, but not always in a way consonant with the thinking of the Church. In fact, there are ideas about salvation and mission which... are focused [exclusively] on humankind's earthly needs. In this view, the Kingdom tends to become something completely human and secularized; what counts are programs and struggles for a liberation which is socio-economic, political, and even cultural, but within a horizon that is closed to the transcendent. Without denying that on this level too there are values to be promoted, such a notion nevertheless remains within the confines of a kingdom of humankind, deprived of its authentic and profound dimensions. Such a view easily translates into [simply] one more ideology of purely earthly progress. The Kingdom of God, however, "is not of this world,... is not from the world" (Jn 18:36).

There are also conceptions which deliberately emphasize the Kingdom and which describe themselves as "Kingdom-centered." They stress the image of a Church which is not concerned about herself, but which is totally concerned with bearing witness to and serving the Kingdom. It is a "Church for others" just as Christ is the "man for others." The Church's task is described as though it had to proceed in two directions: on the one hand promoting such "values of the Kingdom" as peace, justice, freedom, brotherhood, etc., while on the other hand fostering dialogue between peoples, cultures, and religions, so that through a mutual enrichment they might help the world to be renewed and to journey ever closer toward the Kingdom.

Together with positive aspects, these conceptions often reveal negative aspects as well. First, they are silent about Christ... since, according to them, Christ cannot be understood by those who lack Christian faith, whereas different peoples, cultures, and religions are capable of finding common ground in the one divine reality, by whatever it is called. For the same reason they put great stress on the mystery of Creation, which is reflected in the diversity of cultures and beliefs, but they keep silent about the mystery of Redemption. Furthermore, the Kingdom, as they understand it, ends up leaving very little room either for the Church or undervaluing the Church....

This is not the Kingdom of God as we know it from [God's] revelation. The Kingdom cannot be detached either from Christ or from the Church. [MR n. 17, 18]

THE WEEK OF MAY 24, 1998

21. THE KINGDOM OF GOD IS A PERSON

Christ not only proclaimed the Kingdom, but in Him the Kingdom itself became present and was fulfilled. This happened not only through His words and deeds: "Above all,... the kingdom is made manifest in the very person of Christ, Son of God and Son of Man, who came 'to serve and to give his life as a ransom for many'" (Mk 10:45).[7]

The Kingdom of God is not a concept, a doctrine, or a program subject to free interpretation, but it is before all else *a person* with the face and name of Jesus of Nazareth, the image of the invisible God. If the Kingdom is separated from Jesus, it is no longer the Kingdom of God which He revealed. The result is a distortion of the meaning of the Kingdom, which runs the risk of being transformed into a purely human or ideological goal, and a distortion of the identity of Christ, who no longer appears as the Lord to whom everything must one day be subjected (see 1 Corinthians 15:27).

Likewise, one may not separate the Kingdom from the Church. It is true that the Church is not an end unto herself, since she is ordered toward the Kingdom of God of which she is the seed, sign, and instrument. Yet, while remaining distinct from Christ and the Kingdom, the Church is indissolubly united to both.

Christ endowed the Church, His Body, with the fullness of the benefits and means of salvation. The Holy Spirit dwells in her, enlivens her with His gifts and charisms, sanctifies, guides, and constantly renews her. The result is a unique and special relationship which—while not excluding the action of Christ and the Spirit outside the Church's visible boundaries—confers upon her a specific and necessary role. Hence the Church's special connection with the Kingdom of God and of Christ, which she has "the mission of announcing and inaugurating among all peoples."[8]

It is within this overall perspective that the reality of the Kingdom is understood. Certainly, the Kingdom demands the promotion of human values, as well as those which can be properly called evangelical, since they are intimately bound up with the "Good News." But this sort of promotion, which is at the heart of the Church, must not be detached from or opposed to other fundamental tasks, such as proclaiming Christ and the Gospel, and establishing and building up communities which make present and active within humankind the living image of the Kingdom. [RM n. 18-19]

22. THE IMPORTANCE OF THE PARISH

The ecclesial community, while always having a universal dimension, finds its most immediate and visible expression in the parish. It is there that the Church is seen locally. In a certain sense it is the Church living in the midst of the homes of her sons and daughters.

It is necessary that in light of the faith all rediscover the true meaning of the parish, that is, the place where the very mystery of the Church is present and at work, even if at times it might be scattered over vast territories or almost not to be found in crowded and chaotic modern sections of cities. The parish is not principally a structure, a territory, or a building, but rather "the family of God, a fellowship afire with a unifying spirit,"[9] "a familial and welcoming home,"[10] the "community of the faithful."[11]

Plainly and simply, the parish is founded on a theological reality because it is a eucharistic community. This means that the parish is a community properly suited for celebrating the Eucharist, the living source for its upbuilding and the sacramental bond of its being in full communion with the whole Church. Such suitableness is rooted in the fact that the parish is a community of faith and an organic community, that is, constituted by the ordained ministers and other Christians, in which the pastor—who represents the diocesan bishop—is the hierarchical bond with the entire particular Church....

In the present circumstances the lay faithful have the ability to do very much and, therefore, ought to do very much toward the growth of an authentic ecclesial communion in their parishes in order to reawaken missionary zeal toward nonbelievers and believers themselves who have abandoned the faith or grown lax in the Christian life.

If indeed the parish is the Church placed in the neighborhoods of humanity, it lives and is at work through being deeply inserted in human society and intimately bound up with its aspirations and its dramatic events. Oftentimes the social context, especially in certain countries and environments, is violently shaken by elements of disintegration and dehumanization. The individual is lost and disoriented, but there always remains in the human heart the desire to experience and cultivate caring and personal relationships.

The response to such a desire can come from the parish, when, with the lay faithful's participation, it adheres to its fundamental vocation and mission, that is, to be a place in the world for the community of believers to gather together as a sign and instrument of the vocation of all to communion: in a word, to be a house of welcome to all and a place of service to all, or, as Pope John XXIII was fond of saying, to be the "village fountain" to which all would have recourse in their thirst. [CL n. 26-27]

23. THE CHURCH NEEDS ONGOING CONVERSION

Only in Christ can men and women find answers to the ultimate questions that trouble them. Only in Christ can they fully understand their dignity as persons created and loved by God. Jesus Christ is "the only Son from the Father... full of grace and truth" (see John 1:14).

By keeping the Incarnation of the eternal Word before her eyes, the Church understands more fully her twofold nature—human and divine. She is the mystical Body of the Word made flesh. As such she is inseparably united with her Lord and is holy in a way that can never fail.

The Church is also the visible means which God uses to reconcile sinful humanity to Himself. She is the people of God making its pilgrim way to the Father's house. In this sense she is constantly in need of conversion and renewal, and her members must ever be challenged "to purify and renew themselves so that the sign of Christ can shine more brightly on [her] face."[12] Only when the Church generates works of genuine holiness and humble service do the words of Isaiah come true: "All nations shall stream toward her" (see Isaiah 2:2). [TPS 39/2, 1994, 89]

THE SACRAMENTS

The Holy Spirit, "the Lord, the Giver of life," gives that divine life of Christ to the Church through the sacraments.

24. THE HOLY SPIRIT AND THE SACRAMENTS

In every celebration of the Eucharist [Christ's] coming, His [saving] presence, is sacramentally realized: in the Sacrifice and in Communion. It is accomplished by the power of the Holy Spirit, as part of His own mission. Through the Eucharist the Holy Spirit accomplishes that "strengthening of the inner man" spoken of in the Letter to the Ephesians (see Ephesians 3:16)....

Through the individual sacraments the Church fulfills her [saving] ministry to man. This sacramental ministry, every time it is accomplished, brings with it the mystery of the departure of Christ through the Cross and the Resurrection, by virtue of which the Holy Spirit comes. He comes and works: He gives life. For the sacraments signify grace and confer grace: they signify life and give life. The Church is the visible dispenser of the sacred signs, while the Holy Spirit acts in them as the invisible dispenser of the life which they signify. Together with the Spirit, Christ Jesus is present and acting. [DV n. 62-63]

25. THE EUCHARIST, CENTER AND SUMMIT OF SACRAMENTAL LIFE

In the mystery of the Redemption, that is to say in Jesus Christ's saving work, the Church not only shares in the Gospel of her Master through fidelity to the word and service of truth, but she also shares, through a submission filled with hope and love, in the power of His redeeming action expressed and enshrined by Him in a sacramental form, especially in the Eucharist. The Eucharist is the center and summit of the whole of sacramental life, through which each Christian receives the saving power of the Redemption, beginning with the mystery of Baptism, in which we are buried into the death of Christ, in order to become sharers in His Resurrection, as the Apostle [Paul] teaches (see Romans 6:3-5).

In the light of this teaching, we see still more clearly the reason why the entire sacramental life of the Church and of each Christian reaches its summit and fullness in the Eucharist. For by Christ's will there is in this sacrament a continual renewing of the mystery of the sacrifice of Himself that Christ offered to the Father on the altar of the Cross. [This is] a sacrifice that the Father accepted, giving, in return for this total self-giving by His Son, who became "obedient unto death" (Phil 2:8), His own paternal gift—that is to say, the grant of new immortal life in the Resurrection, since the Father is the first Source and the Giver of life from the beginning. That new life, which involves the bodily glorification of the crucified Christ, became an efficacious sign of the new gift granted to humanity, the gift that is the Holy Spirit, through whom the divine life that the Father has in Himself and gives to His Son (see John 5:26; 1 John 5:11) is communicated to all men who are united with Christ. [RH n. 20]

26. THE CHURCH LIVES BY THE EUCHARIST

The Church lives by the Eucharist, by the fullness of this sacrament, the stupendous content and meaning of which have often been expressed in the Church's Magisterium from the most distant times down to our own days. However, we can say with certainty that—although this teaching is sustained by the acuteness of theologians, by men of deep faith and prayer, and by ascetics and mystics, in complete fidelity to the eucharistic mystery—it still reaches no more than the threshold.... [I]t is incapable of grasping and translating into words what the Eucharist is in all its fullness, what is expressed by it, and what is actuated by it.

Indeed, the Eucharist is the ineffable sacrament! The essential commitment and, above all, the visible grace and source of supernatural strength for the Church as the people of God is to persevere and advance constantly in eucharistic life and eucharistic piety and to develop spiritually in the climate of the Eucharist.

With all the greater reason, then, it is not permissible for us, in thought, life, or action, to take away from this truly most holy sacrament its full magnitude and its essential meaning. It is at one and the same time a Sacrifice-sacrament, a Communion-sacrament, and a Presence-sacrament. And, although it is true that the Eucharist always was and must continue to be the most profound revelation of the human brotherhood of Christ's disciples and confessors, it cannot be treated merely as an occasion for manifesting this brotherhood. When celebrating the sacrament of the Body and Blood of the Lord, the full magnitude of the divine mystery must be respected—as must the full meaning of this sacramental sign in which Christ is really present and is received, the soul is filled with grace, and the pledge of future glory is given. [RH n. 20]

27. THE EUCHARIST AND THE KINGDOM

The Kingdom of God becomes present above all in the celebration of the sacrament of the Eucharist, which is the Lord's Sacrifice. In that celebration the fruits of the earth and the work of human hands—the bread and wine—are transformed mysteriously, but really and substantially, through the power of the Holy Spirit and the words of the minister, into the Body and Blood of the Lord Jesus Christ, the Son of God and Son of Mary, through whom the Kingdom of the Father has been made present in our midst.

The goods of this world and the work of our hands—the bread and wine—serve for the coming of the definitive Kingdom, since the Lord, through His Spirit, takes them up into Himself in order to offer Himself to the Father and to offer us with Himself in the renewal of His one Sacrifice, which anticipates God's Kingdom and proclaims its final coming.

Thus the Lord unites us with Himself through the Eucharist—Sacrament and Sacrifice—and He unites us with Himself and with one another by a bond stronger than any natural union.... Thus united, He sends us into the whole world to bear witness, through faith and works, to God's love, preparing the coming of His Kingdom and anticipating it, though in the obscurity of the present time. [SRS n. 48]

28. EUCHARISTIC WORSHIP LEADS TO CHARITY

Eucharistic worship constitutes the soul of all

Christian life. In fact, Christian life is expressed in the fulfilling of the greatest commandment, that is to say, in the love of God and neighbor, and this love finds its source in the Blessed Sacrament, which is commonly called the Sacrament of Love.

The Eucharist signifies this charity, and therefore recalls it, makes it present, and at the same time brings it about. Every time that we consciously share in it, there opens in our souls a real dimension of that unfathomable love that includes everything that God has done and continues to do for us human beings, as Christ says: "My Father goes on working, and so do I" (see John 5:17).

Together with this unfathomable and free gift, which is charity revealed in its fullest degree in the saving sacrifice of the Son of God—the sacrifice of which the Eucharist is the indelible sign—there also springs up within us a lively response of love. We not only know love; we ourselves begin to love. We enter, so to speak, upon the path of love and along this path make progress.

Thanks to the Eucharist, the love that springs up within us from the Eucharist develops in us, becomes deeper and grows stronger. Eucharistic worship is therefore precisely the expression of that love which is the authentic and deepest characteristic of the Christian vocation. This worship springs from the love and serves the love to which we are all called in Jesus Christ.

A living fruit of this worship is the perfecting of the image of God that we bear within us, an image that corresponds to the one that Christ has revealed in us. As we thus become adorers of the Father "in spirit and truth" (Jn 4:23), we mature in an ever-fuller union with Christ, we are ever more united to Him, and—if one may use the expression—we are ever more in harmony with Him. [DC n. 5]

29. THE EUCHARIST, SCHOOL OF LOVE

The authentic sense of the Eucharist becomes of itself the school of active love for neighbor. We know that this is the true and full order of love that the Lord has taught us: "By this love you have for one another, everyone will know that you are my disciples" (see John 13:35). The Eucharist educates us to this love in a deeper way; it shows us, in fact, what value each person, our brother or sister, has in God's eyes, if Christ offers Himself equally to each one, under the species of bread and wine. If our eucharistic worship is authentic, it must make us grow in awareness of the dignity of each person. The awareness of that dignity becomes the deepest motive of our relationship with our neighbor.

We must also become particularly sensitive to all human suffering and misery, to all injustice and wrong, and seek the way to redress them effectively. Let us learn to discover with respect the truth about the inner self that becomes the dwelling place of God in the Eucharist. Christ comes into the hearts of our brothers and sisters and visits their consciences.

How the image of each and every one changes when we become aware of this reality, when we make it the subject of our reflections! The sense of the eucharistic mystery leads us to a love for our neighbor, to a love for every human being. [DC n. 6]

UNITY IN THE CHURCH

Reflection on the Spirit of love, who has been poured out on every member of the Church, should lead us to ponder how we can allow His love to overcome divisions within the Church.

THE WEEK OF JULY 26, 1998

30. CATHOLIC UNITY

The reflection of the faithful in the second year of preparation ought to focus particularly on the value of unity within the Church, to which the various gifts and charisms bestowed upon her by the Spirit are directed.... The unity of the Body of Christ is founded on the activity of the Spirit, guaranteed by the apostolic ministry and sustained by mutual love (see 1 Corinthians 13:1-8). This catechetical enrichment of the faith cannot fail to bring the members of the p eople of God to a more mature awareness of their own responsibilities, as well as to a more lively sense of the importance of ecclesial obedience. [TMA n. 47]

THE WEEK OF AUGUST 2, 1998

31. A CREDIBLE SIGN OF RECONCILIATION

United to Christ as a visible communion of persons, the Church must take as her model the early Christian community in Jerusalem, which devoted itself "to the apostles' teaching and fellowship, to the breaking of bread and the prayers" (Acts 2:42). If the Church is to be a credible sign of reconciliation to the world, all those who believe, whoever they may be, must be "of one heart and one soul" (Acts 4:32).

By your fraternal communion the world will know that you are Christ's disciples!

The members of the Catholic Church should take to heart the plea of St. Paul: always be "eager to maintain the unity of the Spirit in the bond of peace" (Eph 4:3). With gentleness and patience, revere the Church as Christ's beloved Bride who is ever vigorous and youthful. So many problems arise when people think of the Church as "theirs," when in fact she belongs to Christ. Christ and the Church are inseparably united as "one flesh" (see Ephesians 5:31). Our love for Christ finds its vital expression in our love for the Church. Polarization and destructive criticism have no place among "those who are of the household of faith" (Gal 6:10). [TPS 39/2, 1994, 89]

THE WEEK OF AUGUST 9, 1998

32. THE MYSTERY OF COMMUNION

We turn to the words of Jesus: "I am the true vine and my Father is the vinedresser.... Abide in me and I in you" (Jn 15:1,4, RSV). These simple words reveal the mystery of communion that serves as the unifying bond between the Lord and His disciples, between Christ and the baptized—a living and life-giving communion through which Christians no longer belong to themselves but are the Lord's very own, as the branches are one with the vine.

The communion of Christians with Jesus has the communion of God as Trinity—namely, the unity of the Son to the Father in the gift of the Holy Spirit—as its model and source, and is itself the means to achieve this communion. United to the Son in the

Spirit's bond of love, Christians are united to the Father.

Jesus continues: "I am the vine, you are the branches" (Jn 15:5). From the communion that Christians experience in Christ there immediately flows the communion which they experience with one another: all are branches of a single vine, namely, Christ. In this communion is the wonderful reflection and participation in the mystery of the intimate life of love in God as Trinity—Father, Son, and Holy Spirit, as revealed by the Lord Jesus. For this communion Jesus prays: "That they may all be one; even as you, Father, are in me, and I in you, that they also may be in us, so that the world may believe that you have sent me" (see John 17:21)....

Church communion then is a gift, a great gift of the Holy Spirit to be gratefully accepted by the lay faithful, and at the same time to be lived with a deep sense of responsibility. This is concretely realized through their participation in the life and mission of the Church, to whose service the lay faithful put their varied and complementary ministries and charisms. [CL n. 18, 20]

33. WE CANNOT REMAIN IN ISOLATION

A member of the lay faithful "can never remain in isolation from the community, but must live in a continual interaction with others, with a lively sense of fellowship, rejoicing in an equal dignity and common commitment to bring to fruition the immense treasure that each has inherited. The Spirit of the Lord gives a vast variety of charisms, inviting people to assume different ministries and forms of service and reminding them, as He reminds all people in their relationship in the Church, that what distinguishes persons is not an increase in dignity, but a special and complementary capacity for service.... Thus, the charisms, the ministries, the different forms of service exercised by the lay faithful exist in communion and on behalf of communion. They are treasures that complement one another for the good of all and are under the wise guidance of their pastors...."[13]

So as to render thanks to God for the great gift of Church communion—which is the reflection in time of the eternal and ineffable communion of the love of God, Three in One—we once again consider Jesus' words: "I am the vine, you are the branches" (Jn 15:5). The awareness of the gift ought to be accompanied by a strong sense of responsibility for its use: it is, in fact, a gift that, like the talent of the Gospel parable, must be put to work in the life of ever-increasing communion.

To be responsible for the gift of communion means, first of all, to be committed to overcoming each temptation to division and opposition that works against the Christian life with its responsibility in the apostolate. The cry of St. Paul continues to resound as a reproach to those who are wounding the Body of Christ: "What I mean is that each one of you says, 'I belong to Paul,' or... 'I belong to Cephas,' or 'I belong to Christ.' Is Christ divided?" (1 Cor 1:12-13).

No, rather let these words of the Apostle sound a persuasive call: "I appeal to you, brethren, by the name of our Lord Jesus Christ, that all of you agree and that there be no dissensions among you, but that you be united in the same mind and the same judgment" (1 Cor 1:10). Thus the life of Church communion will become a sign for all the world and a compelling force that will lead persons to faith in Christ: "That they may all be one; even as you, Father, are in me and I in you, that they also may be in us, so that the world may believe that you have sent me" (see John 17:21). In such a way communion leads to *mission,* and mission itself to communion. [CL n. 20]

34. PATHS TO UNITY IN THE CHURCH

In order to overcome conflicts and to ensure that normal tensions do not prove harmful to the unity of the Church, we must all apply ourselves to the Word of God. We must relinquish our own subjective views and seek the truth where it is to be found, namely in the Divine Word itself and in the authentic interpretation of that Word provided by the Magisterium of the Church. In this light, listening to one another; respect; refraining from all hasty judgments; patience; the ability to avoid subordinating the faith which unites to the opinions, fashions, and ideological choices which divide—these are all qualities of a dialogue within the Church which must be persevering, open, and sincere.

Obviously dialogue would not have these qualities and would not become a factor of reconciliation if the magisterium were not heeded and accepted. Thus actively engaged in seeking her own internal communion, the Catholic Church can address an appeal for reconciliation to the other churches with which there does not exist full communion, as well as to the other religions and even to all those who are seeking God with a sincere heart. [RP n. 25]

THE WEEK OF AUGUST 30, 1998

35. UNITY IS THE FRUIT OF CONVERSION

Unity is not the result of human policies or hidden and mysterious intentions. Instead, unity springs from conversion of the heart, and from sincere acceptance of the unchanging principles laid down by Christ for His Church. Particularly important among these principles is the effective communion of all the parts of the Church with her visible foundation: Peter, the Rock.

Consequently, a Catholic who wishes to remain such and to be recognized as such cannot reject the principle of communion with the successor of Peter. [TPS 40/3, 1995, 160]

CLERGY, RELIGIOUS, AND LAITY

The Holy Spirit has given different but complementary charisms and ministries to those in each state of the Christian life; all of them are necessary for the Church to fulfill her mission.

THE WEEK OF SEPTEMBER 6, 1998

36. A DIVERSITY OF GIFTS

All the members of the people of God—clergy, men and women religious, the lay faithful—are laborers in the vineyard... Every one of us possessing charisms and ministries, diverse yet complementary, works in the one and the same vineyard of the Lord. Simply in *being* Christians, even before actually *doing* the works of a Christian, all are branches of the one fruitful vine which is Christ. All are living members of the one Body of the Lord built up through the power of the Spirit....

The states of life, by being ordered one to the other, are thus bound together among themselves. They all share in a deeply basic meaning: that of being the manner of living out the commonly shared Christian dignity and the universal call to holiness in the perfection of love. They are different yet complementary in the sense that each of them has a basic and unmistakable character which sets each apart, while at the same time each of them is seen in relation to the other and placed at each other's service.

Thus the *lay* state of life has its distinctive feature in its secular character. It fulfills an ecclesial service in bearing witness and, in its own way, recalling for priests [and] women and men religious the significance of the earthly and temporal realities in the [saving] plan of God. In turn, the *ministerial* priesthood represents, in different times and places, the permanent guarantee of the sacramental presence of Christ the Redeemer. The *religious* state bears witness to the . . . straining toward the Kingdom of God that is prefigured and in some way anticipated and experienced even now through the vows of chastity, poverty, and obedience.

All the states of life, whether taken collectively or individually in relation to the others, are at the service of the Church's growth. While different in expression they are deeply united in the Church's mystery of communion and are dynamically coordinated in its unique mission. Thus in the diversity of the states of life and the variety of vocations this same unique mystery of the Church reveals and experiences anew the infinite richness of the mystery of Jesus Christ. [CL n. 55]

37. PRAY AND WORK FOR VOCATIONS

"I will give you shepherds after my own heart" (Jer 3:15). Today, this promise of God is still living and at work in the Church. At all times, she knows she is the fortunate receiver of these prophetic words. She sees them put into practice daily in so many parts of the world, or rather, in so many human hearts, young hearts in particular. On the threshold of the third millennium, and in the face of the serious and urgent needs which confront the Church and the world, she yearns to see this promise fulfilled in a new and richer way, more intensely and effectively. She hopes for an extraordinary outpouring of the Spirit of Pentecost.

The Lord's promise calls forth from the heart of the Church a prayer that is a confident and burning petition in the love of the Father, who—just as He has sent Jesus the Good Shepherd, the Apostles, their successors, and a countless host of priests—will continue to show to the people of today his faithfulness, his goodness.

And the Church is ready to respond to this grace. She feels in her heart that God's gift begs for a united and generous reply. The entire people of God should pray and work tirelessly for priestly vocations. Candidates for the priesthood should prepare themselves very conscientiously to welcome God's gift and put it into practice, knowing that the Church and the world have an absolute need of them. They should deepen their love for Christ the Good Shepherd, pattern their hearts on His, be ready to go out as His image into the highways of the world to proclaim to all mankind Christ the Way, the Truth, and the Life.

I appeal especially to families. May parents, mothers in particular, be generous in giving their sons to the Lord when He calls them to the priesthood. May they cooperate joyfully in their vocational journey, realizing that in this way they will be increasing and deepening their Christian fruitfulness in the Church and that, in a sense, they will experience the blessedness of Mary, the Virgin Mother: "Blessed are you among women, and blessed is the fruit of your womb!" (Lk 1:42).

To today's young people I say: Be docile to the voice of the Spirit, let the great expectations of the Church, of mankind, resound in the depths of your hearts. Do not be afraid to open your minds to Christ the Lord who is calling. Feel His loving look upon you and respond enthusiastically to Jesus when He asks you to follow Him without reserve. [PDV n. 82]

THE WEEK OF SEPTEMBER 20, 1998

38. THE CLERGY: A GRACE FOR THE WHOLE CHURCH

The ministries which exist and are at work at this time in the Church are all—even in their variety of forms—a participation in Jesus Christ's own ministry as the Good Shepherd who lays down His life for the sheep (see John 10:11), the humble servant who gives Himself without reserve for the salvation of all (see Mark 10:45). The Apostle Paul is quite clear in speaking about the ministerial constitution of the Church in apostolic times. In his First Letter to the Corinthians he writes: "And God has appointed in the Church first apostles, second prophets, third teachers..." (1 Cor 12:28)....

In a primary position in the Church are the ordained ministries, that is, the ministries that come from the Sacrament of Orders. In fact, with the mandate to make disciples of all nations (see Matthew 28:19), the Lord Jesus chose and constituted the Apostles—seed of the People of the New Covenant and origin of the hierarchy—to form and to rule the priestly people. The mission of the Apostles, which the Lord Jesus continues to entrust to the pastors of His people, is a true service, significantly referred to in Sacred Scripture as... service or ministry.

The ministries receive the charism of the Holy Spirit from the risen Christ in uninterrupted succession from the Apostles, through the Sacrament of Orders. From Him they receive the authority and sacred power to serve the Church, acting... in the person of Christ, the Head, and to gather her in the Holy Spirit through the Gospel and the sacraments.

The ordained ministries, apart from the persons who receive them, are a grace for the entire Church. These ministries express and realize a participation in the priesthood of Jesus Christ that is different, not simply in degree but in essence, from the participation given to all the lay faithful through Baptism and Confirmation. On the other hand, the ministerial priesthood... essentially has the royal priesthood of all the faithful as its aim and is ordered to it.

For this reason, so as to assure and to increase communion in the Church, particularly in those places where there is a diversity and complementarity of ministries, pastors must always acknowledge that their ministry is fundamentally ordered to the service of the entire people of God (see Hebrews 5:1). The lay faithful, in turn, must acknowledge that the ministerial priesthood is totally necessary for their participation in the mission of the Church.

The Church's mission of salvation in the world is realized not only by the ministers in virtue of the Sacrament of Orders but also by all the lay faithful.... The pastors, therefore, ought to acknowledge and foster the ministries, the offices, and roles of the lay faithful that find their foundation in the Sacraments of Baptism and Confirmation, indeed, for a good many of them, in the Sacrament of Matrimony. [CL n. 21-22]

THE WEEK OF SEPTEMBER 27, 1998

39. PRIESTS REPRESENT CHRIST

Priests are called to prolong the presence of Christ, the one high priest, embodying His way of life and making Him visible in the midst of the flock entrusted to their care. We find this clearly and precisely stated in the First Letter of Peter: "I exhort the elders among you as a fellow elder and a witness of the sufferings of Christ as well as a partaker in the glory that is to be revealed. Tend the flock of God that is your

117

charge, not by constraint but willingly, not for shameful gain but eagerly, not as domineering over those in your charge but being examples to the flock. And when the Chief Shepherd is manifested you will obtain the unfading crown of glory" (1 Pt 5:1-4).

In the Church and on behalf of the Church, priests are a sacramental representation of Jesus Christ—the Head and Shepherd—authoritatively proclaiming His word, repeating His acts of forgiveness and His offer of salvation, particularly in Baptism, Penance, and the Eucharist, showing His loving concern to the point of a total gift of self for the flock, which they gather into unity and lead to the Father through Christ and in the Spirit. In a word, priests exist and act in order to proclaim the Gospel to the world and to build up the Church in the name and person of Christ the Head and Shepherd.

This is the ordinary and proper way in which ordained ministers share in the one priesthood of Christ. By the sacramental anointing of Holy Orders, the Holy Spirit configures them in a new and special way to Jesus Christ the Head and Shepherd. He forms and strengthens them with His pastoral charity. And He gives them an authoritative role in the Church as servants of the proclamation of the Gospel to every people and of the fullness of Christian life of all the baptized. [PDV n. 15-16]

THE WEEK OF OCTOBER 4, 1998
40. ON THE SHORTAGE OF PRIESTS
Our times consume and require ever-greater priestly energy. However, although many parts of the world

are experiencing a great blossoming of vocations, in other areas one notices a persistent shortage of priests and the phenomenon of a great many sacred ministers of advanced age, ill, or worn out by the evermore whirling pace of apostolic ministry. As a result, even where the number of ordinations and seminarians has increased, the availability of priests is still insufficient to meet all needs.

Hence the demand is felt for an appropriate collaboration of the lay faithful in the pastoral ministry of priests, while always respecting, logically, the sacramental limits and the difference of charisms and ecclesial roles.... [But] the particular gift of each of the Church's members must be wisely and carefully acknowledged, safeguarded, promoted, discerned, and coordinated, without confusing roles, functions, or theological or canonical status. Otherwise the Body of Christ is not built up nor does its mission of salvation correctly develop.... We cannot increase the communion and unity of the Church by clericalizing the lay faithful or by laicizing priests.

As a consequence, we cannot offer the lay faithful experiences and ways of participating in the pastoral ministry of priests that would in any way or to any degree entail a theoretical or practical misconception of the unchangeable differences willed by Christ and the Holy Spirit for the good of the Church: the diversity of vocations and states of life, the diversity of ministries, charisms, and responsibilities.... It should also be understood that these clarifications and distinctions do not stem from a concern to defend clerical privileges, but from the need to be obedient to the will of Christ and to respect the constitutive form which He indelibly impressed on His Church....

Above all, it must never be forgotten that problems caused by the shortage of ordained ministers can be alleviated only secondarily or temporarily by having lay people in some way supply for them. The shortage of sacred ministers can be avoided only by "praying the Lord of the harvest to send out laborers into his harvest" (see Matthew 9:38), giving the primacy to God and caring for the identity and holiness of the priests there are. This is simply the logic of faith! Every Christian community that lives its total dedication to Christ and remains open to His grace will obtain from Him precisely those vocations which serve to represent Him as the Shepherd of His people.

Where there is a shortage of these vocations, the essential problem is not to search for alternatives—and God forbid that they should be sought by distorting His wise plan—but to focus all the efforts of the Christian people on making the voice of Christ, who never stops calling, heard again in families, parishes, Catholic schools, and communities. [TPS 39/5, 1994, 309-12]

THE WEEK OF OCTOBER 11, 1998

41. PRIESTS WILL CONTINUE TO THE END OF TIME

There is an essential aspect of the priest that does not change: the priest of tomorrow, no less than the priest of today, must resemble Christ. When Jesus lived on this earth, He manifested in Himself the definitive role of the priest by establishing a ministerial priesthood with which the Apostles were the first to be invested. This priesthood is destined to last in endless succession throughout history.

In this sense, the priest of the third millennium will continue the work of the priests who, in the preceding millennia, have animated the life of the Church. In the third millennium the priestly vocation will continue to be the call to live the unique and permanent priesthood of Christ. [PDV n. 5]

42. THE LAY FAITHFUL: CALLED TO HOLINESS

We come to a full sense of the dignity of the lay faithful if we consider the prime and fundamental vocation that the Father assigns to each of them in Jesus Christ through the Holy Spirit: the vocation to holiness, that is, the perfection of charity. Holiness is the greatest testimony of the dignity conferred on a disciple of Christ....

The Church... is the choice vine whose branches live and grow with the same holy and life-giving energies that come from Christ. She is the Mystical Body whose members share in the same life of holiness of the Head who is Christ. She is the beloved spouse of the Lord Jesus who delivered Himself up for her sanctification (see Ephesians 5:25ff). The Spirit that sanctified the human nature of Jesus in Mary's virginal womb (see Luke 1:35) is the same Spirit that is abiding and working in the Church to communicate to her the holiness of the Son of God made man.

It is evermore urgent that today all Christians take up again the way of the Gospel renewal, welcoming in a spirit of generosity the invitation expressed by the Apostle Peter "to be holy in all conduct" (see 1

Peter 1:15).... Everyone in the Church, precisely because they are members, receives and thereby shares in the common vocation to holiness. In the fullness of this title and on equal par with all other members of the Church, the lay faithful are called to holiness....

The call to holiness is rooted in Baptism and proposed anew in the other sacraments, principally in the Eucharist. Since Christians are reclothed in Christ Jesus and refreshed by His Spirit, they are "holy." They therefore have the ability to manifest this holiness and the responsibility to bear witness to it in all that they do. The Apostle Paul never tires of admonishing all Christians to live "as is fitting among saints" (Eph 5:3).

Life according to the Spirit, whose fruit is holiness (see Romans 6:22; Galatians 5:22), stirs up every baptized person and requires each to follow and imitate Jesus Christ in embracing the Beatitudes; in listening and meditating on the Word of God; in conscious and active participation in the liturgical and sacramental life of the Church; in personal prayer; in family or in community; in the hunger and thirst for justice; in the practice of the commandment of love in all circumstances of life and service to the brethren, especially the least, the poor, and the suffering. [CL n. 16]

43. THE CHARISMS OF THE HOLY SPIRIT

The Holy Spirit, while bestowing diverse ministries in Church communion, enriches it still further with particular gifts or promptings of grace, called *charisms.* These can take a great variety of forms both as a manifestation of the absolute freedom of the Spirit who abundantly supplies them and as a response to the varied needs of the Church in history. The description and the classification given to these gifts in the New Testament are an indication of their rich variety.

"To each [writes the Apostle Paul] is given the manifestation of the Spirit for the common good. To one is given through the Spirit the utterance of wisdom, and to another the utterance of knowledge according to the same Spirit, to another faith by the same Spirit, to another gifts of healing by the one Spirit, to another the working of miracles, to another prophecy, to another the ability to distinguish between spirits, to another various kinds of tongues, to another the interpretation of tongues" (1 Cor 12:7-10; see also 12:4-6, 28-31; Romans 12:6-8; 1 Peter 4:10-11).

Whether they be exceptional and great or simple and ordinary, the charisms are graces of the Holy Spirit that have, directly or indirectly, a usefulness for the ecclesial community, ordered as they are to the building up of the Church, to the well-being of humanity, and to the needs of the world.

Even in our own times there is no lack of a fruitful manifestation of various charisms among the faithful, women and men. These charisms are given to individual persons and can be shared by others in such ways as to continue in time a precious and effective heritage, serving as a source of a particular spiritual affinity among persons....

The gifts of the Spirit demand that those who have received them exercise them for the growth of the whole Church. The charisms are received in gratitude both on the part of the one who receives them and also on the part of the entire Church. They are in fact a singularly rich source of grace for the vitality of the apostolate and for the holiness of the whole Body of Christ, provided that they be gifts that come truly from the Spirit and are exercised in full conformity with the authentic promptings of the Spirit. In this sense the discernment of charisms is always necessary....No charism dispenses a person from reference and submission to the pastors of the Church. [CL n. 24]

44. LAY PARTICIPATION AND COOPERATION IN CHURCH AFFAIRS

Lay people, "by reason of the knowledge, competence, or outstanding ability which they enjoy, are able and sometimes even obliged to express their opinion on things which concern the good of the Church."[14] They can do this either individually or through appropriate bodies. It is therefore incumbent upon the Church's pastors to be attentive to the suggestions and proposals of the lay faithful, while at the same time exercising the freedom and authority which is theirs by divine right to shepherd that part of God's people entrusted to them.

It would be an error to judge ecclesial structures of participation and cooperation by secular democratic standards, or to consider them as forms of "power-sharing" or means of imposing partisan ideas or interests. They should be looked on as forms of spiritual solidarity proper to the Church as a communion of persons who, "though many, are one body in Christ, and individually members one of another" (Rom 12:5). Such structures are fruitful to the extent that they manifest the true nature of the Church as a hierarchical communion, animated and guided by the Holy Spirit. [TPS 39/2, 1994, 122]

EVANGELIZATION AND MISSION

Christ promised to pour out the Holy Spirit upon His followers so that they would "receive power" for the mission He had given them: to be His "witnesses… to the end of the earth" (Acts 1:8).

THE WEEK OF NOVEMBER 8, 1998

45. THE URGENCY OF MISSIONARY ACTIVITY

The mission of Christ the Redeemer, which is entrusted to the Church, is still very far from completion. As the second millennium after Christ's coming draws to an end, an overall view of the human race shows that this mission is still only beginning and that we must commit ourselves wholeheartedly to its service. It is the Spirit who impels us to proclaim the great works of God: "For if I preach the Gospel, that gives me no ground for boasting. For necessity is laid upon me. Woe to me if I do not preach the Gospel!" (1 Cor 9:16)….

There is a new awareness that missionary activity is a matter for all Christians, for all dioceses and parishes, Church institutions and associations. Nevertheless, in this new springtime of Christianity there is an undeniable negative tendency.... Missionary activity specifically directed "to the nations" (*ad gentes*) appears to be waning, and this tendency is certainly not in line with the directives of the [Second Vatican] Council and of subsequent statements of the Magisterium. Difficulties both internal and external have weakened the Church's missionary thrust toward non-Christians, a fact which must arouse concern among all who believe in Christ. For in the Church's history, missionary drive has always been a sign of vitality, just as its lessening is a sign of a crisis of faith....

I wish to invite the Church to renew her missionary commitment.... For missionary activity renews the Church, revitalizes faith and Christian identity, and offers fresh enthusiasm and new incentive. Faith is strengthened when it is given to others! It is in commitment to the Church's universal mission that the new evangelization of Christian peoples will find inspiration and support.

But what moves me even more strongly to proclaim the urgency of missionary evangelization is the fact that it is the primary service which the Church can render to every individual and to all humanity in the modern world, a world which has experienced marvelous achievements but which seems to have lost its sense of ultimate realities and of existence itself....

Peoples everywhere, open the doors to Christ! His Gospel in no way detracts from the human person's freedom, from the respect that is owed to every culture, and to whatever is good in each religion. By accepting Christ, you open yourselves to the definitive Word of God, to the One in whom God has made Himself fully known and has shown us the path to Himself. [RM n. 1-3]

46. NEW OPPORTUNITIES FOR EVANGELIZATION

The number of those who do not know Christ and do not belong to the Church is constantly on the increase. Indeed, since the end of the [Second Vatican] Council it has almost doubled. When we consider this immense portion of humanity which is loved by the Father and for whom He sent His Son, the urgency of the Church's mission is obvious.

On the other hand, our own times offer the Church new opportunities in this field. We have witnessed the collapse of oppressive ideologies and political systems; the opening of frontiers and the formation of a more united world due to an increase in communications; the affirmation among peoples of the Gospel values which Jesus made incarnate in His own life (peace, justice, brotherhood, concern for the needy); and a kind of soulless economic and technical development which only stimulates the search for the truth about God, about man, and about the meaning of life itself.

God is opening before the Church the horizons of a humanity more fully prepared for the sowing of the Gospel. I sense that the moment has come to commit all of the Church's energies to a new evangelization and to the mission *ad gentes*. No believer in Christ, no institution of the Church, can avoid this supreme duty: to proclaim Christ to all peoples. [RM 3]

47. LAY HOLINESS AND LAY MISSION

The vocation of the lay faithful to holiness implies that life according to the Spirit expresses itself in a particular way in their involvement in temporal affairs and in their participation in earthly activities. Once again the Apostle admonishes us: "Whatever you do, in word or deed, do everything in the name of the Lord Jesus, giving thanks to God the Father through him" (Col 3:17)....

The vocation to holiness must be recognized and lived by the lay faithful, first of all as an undeniable and demanding obligation and as a shining example of the infinite love of the Father that has regenerated them in His own life of holiness. Such a vocation, then, ought to be called an essential and inseparable element of the new life of Baptism, and therefore an element which determines their dignity. At the same time the vocation to holiness is intimately connected to mission and to the responsibility entrusted to the lay faithful in the Church and in the world. In fact, that same holiness, which is derived simply from their participation in the Church's holiness, represents their first and fundamental contribution to the building of the Church herself, who is the "Communion of Saints."

The eyes of faith behold a wonderful scene: that of a countless number of lay people, both women and men, busy at work in their daily life and activity, oftentimes far from view and quite unacclaimed by the world, unknown to the world's great personages but nonetheless looked upon in love by the Father, untiring laborers who work in the Lord's vineyard.

Confident and steadfast through the power of God's grace, these are the humble yet great builders of the Kingdom of God in history. [CL n. 17]

48. SHARERS IN CHRIST'S MISSION

The lay faithful are sharers in the *priestly mission* for which Jesus offered Himself on the Cross and continues to be offered in the celebration of the Eucharist for the glory of God and the salvation of humanity. Incorporated in Jesus Christ, the baptized are united to Him and to His sacrifice in the offering they make of themselves and their daily activities (see Romans 12:1-2)....

Through their participation in the *prophetic mission* of Christ, "who proclaimed the kingdom of his Father by the testimony of his life and by the power of his word,"[15] the lay faithful are given the ability and responsibility to accept the Gospel in faith and to proclaim it in word and deed, without hesitating to courageously identify and denounce evil. United to Christ, the "great prophet" (Luke 7:16), and in the Spirit made witnesses of the risen Christ, the lay faithful are made sharers in the appreciation of the Church's supernatural faith, that "cannot err in matters of belief,"[16] and sharers as well in the grace of the Word (see Acts 2:17-18; Revelation 19:10). They are also called to allow the newness and the power of the Gospel to shine out every day in their family and social life, as well as to express patiently and courageously in the contradictions of the present age their hope of future glory even "through the framework of their secular life."[17]

Because the lay faithful belong to Christ, Lord and King of the Universe, they share in His *kingly mis-sion* and are called by Him to spread that Kingdom in history. They exercise their kingship as Christians, above all in the spiritual combat in which they seek to overcome in themselves the kingdom of sin (see Romans 6:12)—and then to make a gift of themselves so as to serve, in justice and in charity, Jesus who is Himself present in all His brothers and sisters, above all in the very least (see Matthew 25:40).

But in particular the lay faithful are called to restore to creation all its original value. In ordering creation to the authentic well-being of humanity in an activity governed by the life of grace, they share in the exercise of the power with which the risen Christ draws all things to Himself and subjects them along with Himself to the Father, so that God might be everything to everyone (see 1 Corinthians 15:28; John 12:32). [CL n. 14-15]

THE WEEK OF DECEMBER 6, 1998

49. EVANGELIZATION IS THE TASK OF EVERY CHRISTIAN

By her very nature the Church is a missionary community. She is continually impelled by this missionary thrust which she has received from the Holy Spirit on the day of Pentecost: "You will receive power when the Holy Spirit comes upon you, and you will be my witnesses" (Acts 1:8, NAB). In fact, the Holy Spirit is the principal agent of the Church's entire mission.

As a consequence, the Christian vocation is also directed toward the apostolate, toward evangelization, toward mission. All baptized persons are called by Christ to become His apostles in their own personal situation and in the world: "As the Father has sent me, so I send you" (Jn 20:21, NAB). Through His Church Christ entrusts you with the fundamental mission of sharing with others the gift of salvation, and He invites you to participate in building His Kingdom. He chooses you, in spite of the personal limitations everyone has, because He loves you and believes in you. This unconditional love of Christ should be the very soul of your apostolic work, in accord with the words of St. Paul: "The love of Christ impels us" (2 Cor 5:14, NAB).

Being disciples of Christ is not a private matter. On the contrary, the gift of faith must be shared with others. For this reason the same Apostle writes, "If I preach the gospel, this is no reason for me to boast, for an obligation has been imposed on me, and woe to me if I do not preach it!" (1 Cor 9:16, NAB). Moreover, do not forget that faith is strengthened and grows precisely when it is given to others.

The mission lands in which you have been called to work are not necessarily located in distant countries, but can be found throughout the world, even in the everyday situations where you are. In the countries of more ancient Christian tradition today there is an urgent need to call attention again to the message of Jesus by means of a new evangelization, since there are widespread groups of people who do not know Christ, or do not know Him well enough. Many, caught by the mechanisms of secularism and religious indifference, are far from Him. [TPS 37/3, 1992, 139-40]

50. PROCLAIMING CHRIST

Proclaiming Christ means above all giving witness to Him with one's life. It is the simplest form of preaching the Gospel and, at the same time, the most effective way available to you. It consists of showing the visible presence of Christ in one's own life by a daily commitment and by making every concrete decision in conformity with the Gospel. Today the world especially needs believable witnesses....

Therefore, testify to your faith through your involvement in the world, too. A disciple of Christ is never a passive and indifferent observer of what is taking place. On the contrary, he feels responsible for transforming social, political, economic, and cultural reality.

Moreover, proclaiming means precisely proclaiming—becoming one who brings the word of salvation to others. There is indeed much ignorance about the Christian faith, but there is also a deep desire to hear the Word of God. And faith comes from listening.

St. Paul writes: "And how can they believe unless they have heard of him?" (see Romans 10:14).... Proclaiming the Word of God is not the responsibility of priests or religious alone, but it is yours, too. You must have the courage to speak about Christ in your families and in places where you study, work, or recreate, inspired with the same fervor the Apostles had when they said, "We cannot help speaking of what we have heard and seen" (see Acts 4:20). Nor should you be silent! There are places and circumstances where you alone can bring the seed of God's word.

Do not be afraid of presenting Christ to someone who does not yet know Him. Christ is the true answer, the most complete answer to all the questions which concern the human person and his destiny. Without Christ, the human person remains an unsolvable riddle. Therefore, have the courage to present Christ! Certainly, you must do this in a way which respects each person's freedom of conscience, but you must do it. Helping a brother or sister to discover Christ, the Way, the Truth, and the Life (see John 14:6), is a true act of love for one's neighbor. [TPS 37/3, 1992, 140-1]

THE WEEK OF DECEMBER 20, 1998

51. WITNESS, THE FIRST FORM OF EVANGELIZATION

People today put more trust in witnesses than in teachers, in experience than in teaching, and in life and action than in theories. The witness of a Christian life is the first and irreplaceable form of mission: Christ, whose mission we continue, is the "witness" *par excellence* (see Revelation 1:5; 3:14) and the model of all Christian witness. The Holy Spirit accompanies the Church along her way and associates her with the witness He gives to Christ (see John 15:26-27).

The first form of witness is the very life of the missionary, of the Christian family, and of the ecclesial community, which reveal a new way of living. The missionary who, despite all his or her human limitations and defects, lives a simple life, taking Christ as the model, is a sign of God and of transcendent realities. But everyone in the Church, striving to imitate the Divine Master, can and must bear this kind of witness; in many cases it is the only possible way of being a missionary.

The evangelical witness which the world finds most appealing is that of concern for people and of charity toward the poor, the weak, and those who suffer. The complete generosity underlying this attitude and these actions stands in marked contrast to human selfishness. It raises precise questions which lead to God and to the Gospel. A commitment to peace, to justice, human rights, and human promotion is also a witness to the Gospel when it is a sign of concern for persons and is directed toward integral human development.

Christians and Christian communities are very much a part of the life of their respective nations and can be a sign of the Gospel in their fidelity to their native land, people, and national culture, while always preserving the freedom brought by Christ.... [But] the Church is [also] called to bear witness to Christ by taking courageous and prophetic stands in the face of the corruption of political or economic power; by not seeking her own glory and material wealth; by using her resources to serve the poorest of the poor and by imitating Christ's own simplicity of life. The Church and her missionaries must also bear the witness of humility, above all with regard to themselves—a humility which allows them to make a personal and communal examination of conscience in order to correct in their behavior whatever is contrary to the Gospel and disfigures the face of Christ. [RM n. 42-43]

52. A NEW MISSIONARY ADVENT

The number of those awaiting Christ is still immense: the human and cultural groups not yet reached by the Gospel, or for whom the Church is scarcely present, are so widespread as to require the uniting of all the Church's resources. As she prepares to celebrate the Jubilee of the year 2000, the whole Church is even more committed to a new missionary advent. We must increase our apostolic zeal to pass on to others the light and joy of the faith, and to this high ideal the whole people of God must be educated.

We cannot be content when we consider the millions of our brothers and sisters, who like us have been redeemed by the blood of Christ, but who live in ignorance of the love of God. For each believer, as for the entire Church, the missionary task must remain foremost, for it concerns the eternal destiny of humanity and corresponds to God's mysterious and merciful plan. [RM n. 86]

1999

YEAR THREE OF PREPARATION:
Returning to God the Father

OUR FATHER, WHO ART IN HEAVEN

God the Father loved the world into being. Though the world has spurned Him, He has sent the Son and the Spirit to call the world back into His loving embrace. As the Father is our beginning, He must also become our destination.

1. A PILGRIMAGE TO THE FATHER'S HOUSE

The third and final year of preparation will be aimed at broadening the horizons of believers, so that they will see things in the perspective of Christ: in the perspective of the "Father who is in heaven" (see Matthew 5:45), from whom the Lord was sent and to whom He has returned (see John 16:28).

"This is eternal life, that they know you the only true God, and Jesus Christ whom you have sent" (see John 17:3). The whole of the Christian life is like a great pilgrimage to the house of the Father, whose unconditional love for every human creature, and in particular for the "prodigal son" (see Luke 15:11-32), we discover anew each day. This pilgrimage takes place in the heart of each person, extends to the believing community, and then reaches to the whole of humanity.

The Jubilee, centered on the person of Christ, thus becomes a great act of praise to the Father: "Blessed be the God and Father of our Lord Jesus Christ, who has blessed us in Christ with every spiritual blessing in the heavenly places, even as he chose us in him before the foundation of the world, that we should be holy and blameless before him" (Eph 1:3-4, RSV). [TMA n. 49]

2. GOD THE FATHER IS LOVE

The Church, as a reconciled and reconciling community, cannot forget that at the source of her gift and mission of reconciliation is the initiative, full of compassionate love and mercy, of that God who is love (see 1 John 4:8) and who out of love created human beings (see Wisdom 11:23-26; Genesis 1:27; Psalms 8:4-8)…. He created them so that they might live in friendship with Him and in communion with one another.

God is faithful to His eternal plan even when man, under the impulse of the evil one (see Wisdom 2:24) and carried away by his own pride, abuses the freedom given to him in order to love and generously seek what is good, and [instead] refuses to obey his Lord and Father. God is faithful even when man, instead of responding with love to God's love, opposes Him and treats Him like a rival, deluding himself and relying on his own power, with the resulting break of relationship with the One who created him. In spite of this transgression on man's part, God remains faithful in love.

It is certainly true that the story of the Garden of Eden makes us think about the tragic consequences of rejecting the Father, which becomes evident in man's inner disorder and in the breakdown of harmony between man and woman, brother and brother (see Genesis 3:12ff; 4:1-16). Also significant is the Gospel parable of the two brothers (the parable of the "prodigal son"; see Luke 15:11-32) who, in different ways, distance themselves from their father and cause a rift between them. Refusal of God's fatherly love and of His loving gifts is always at the root of humanity's divisions.

But we know that God, "rich in mercy" (Eph 2:4), like the father in the parable [of the prodigal son], does not close His heart to any of His children. He waits for them, looks for them, goes to meet them at the place where the refusal of communion imprisons them in isolation and division. He calls them to gather about His table in the joy of the feast of forgiveness and reconciliation.

This initiative on God's part is made concrete and manifest in the redemptive act of Christ, which radiates through the world by means of the ministry of the Church. [RP n. 10]

THE WEEK OF JANUARY 17, 1999

3. THE FATHER OF MERCY

Revelation and faith teach us not only to meditate in the abstract upon the mystery of God as "Father of mercies," but also to have recourse to that mercy in the name of Christ and in union with Him. Did not Christ say that our Father, who "sees in secret" (Mt 6:4, 6, 18), is always waiting for us to have recourse to Him in every need and always waiting for us to study His mystery—the mystery of the Father and His love? (see Ephesians 3:18, Luke 11:5-13)....

Although God "dwells in unapproachable light" (1 Tm 6:16, RSV), He speaks to man by means of the whole of the universe: "ever since the creation of the world his invisible nature, namely, His eternal power and deity, has been clearly perceived in the things that have been made" (Rom 1:20). This indirect and imperfect knowledge, achieved by the intellect seeking God by means of creatures through the visible world, [nevertheless] falls short of [a] vision of the

Father. "No one has ever seen God," writes St. John, in order to stress the truth that "the only Son, who is in the bosom of the Father, He has made Him known" (Jn 1:18).

This "making known" [of the Father by Christ] reveals God in the most profound mystery of His being, one and three, surrounded by "unapproachable light...." Through this "making known" by Christ, we know God above all in His relationship of love for man.... It is precisely here that "His invisible nature" becomes in a special way "visible," incomparably more visible than through all the other "things that have been made": it becomes visible in Christ and through Christ, through His actions and His words, and finally through His death on the Cross and His resurrection. [DM n. 2]

THE VIRTUE OF LOVE
The Father has created us out of the superabundance of his love, and "whoever loves is born of God and knows God" (see 1 John 4:7).

THE WEEK OF JANUARY 24, 1999

4. MAN, THE IMAGE OF THE GOD WHO IS LOVE

God created man in His own image and likeness (see Genesis 1:26-27): Calling him to existence through love, He called him at the same time for love.

God is love (see 1 John 4:8) and in Himself He lives a mystery of personal loving communion. Creating the human race in His own image and continually keeping it in being, God inscribed in the humanity of man and woman the vocation, and thus the capacity and responsibility, of love and communion. Love is therefore the fundamental and innate vocation of every human being. [FC n. 11]

The vocation to love, understood as true openness to our fellow human beings and solidarity with them, is the most basic of all vocations. It is the origin of all vocations in life. That is what Jesus was looking for in the young man when He said: "Keep the commandments" (see Mark 10:19).

In other words: Serve God and your neighbor according to all the demands of a true and upright heart. And when the young man indicated that he was already following that path, Jesus invited him to an even greater love: Leave all and come, follow Me; leave everything that concerns only yourself and join Me in the immense task of saving the world (see verse 21). Along the path of each person's existence, the Lord has something for each one to do. [TPS 40/3, 1995, 162]

THE WEEK OF JANUARY 31, 1999

5. IMITATE JESUS' LOVE

Jesus asks us to follow Him and to imitate Him along the path of love, a love which gives itself completely to the brethren out of love for God: "This is my commandment, that you love one another as I have loved you" (Jn 15:12). The word "as" requires imitation of Jesus and of His love, of which the washing of feet is a sign: "If I, then, your Lord and Teacher, have washed your feet, you also ought to wash one another's feet. For I have given you an example, that

you also should do as I have done to you" (Jn 13:14-
15).

Jesus' way of acting and His words, His deeds, and
His precepts constitute the moral rule of Christian
life. Indeed, His actions, and in particular His
Passion and death on the Cross, are the living Revelation of His love for the Father and for others. This is
exactly the love that Jesus wishes to be imitated by all
who follow Him. It is the "new" commandment: "A
new commandment I give to you, that you love one
another; even as I have loved you, that you also love
one another. By this all men will know that you are
my disciples, if you have love for one another" (Jn
13:34-35)....

To imitate and live out the love of Christ is not
possible for man by his own strength alone. He
becomes capable of this love only by virtue of a gift
received. As the Lord Jesus receives the love of His
Father, so He in turn freely communicates that love
to His disciples: "As the Father has loved me, so have
I loved you; abide in my love" (Jn 15:9). Christ's gift
is His Spirit, whose first "fruit" (Gal 5:22) is charity:
"God's love has been poured into our hearts through
the Holy Spirit which has been given to us" (Rom
5:5).

St. Augustine asks, "Does love bring about the
keeping of the commandments or does the keeping
of the commandments bring about love?" And he
answers, "But who can doubt that love comes first?
For the one who does not love has no reason for
keeping the commandments...."[1]

Love and life according to the Gospel cannot be
thought of first and foremost as a kind of precept,

because what they demand is beyond man's abilities. They are possible only as the result of a gift of God who heals, restores, and transforms the human heart by His grace: "For the law was given through Moses; grace and truth came through Jesus Christ" (Jn 1:17). [VS n. 20, 22-23]

MARY, MODEL OF LOVE
Jesus has commended the Church to the love of His Blessed Mother, who invites us to return to the house of the Father.

THE WEEK OF FEBRUARY 7, 1999

6. A MOTHER'S INEXHAUSTIBLE LOVE

We can say that the mystery of the Redemption took shape beneath the heart of the Virgin of Nazareth when she pronounced her "fiat" ["let it be done"]. From then on, under the special influence of the Holy Spirit, this heart, the heart of both a virgin and a mother, has always followed the work of her Son and has gone out to all those whom Christ has embraced and continues to embrace with inexhaustible love. For that reason her heart must also have the inexhaustibility of a mother.

The special characteristic of the motherly love that the Mother of God inserts in the mystery of the Redemption and the life of the Church finds expression in its exceptional closeness to man and all that happens to him. It is in this that the mystery of the Mother consists. The Church, which looks to her with altogether special love and hope, wishes to make this mystery her own in an ever-deeper manner.... The

Father's eternal love, which has been manifested in the history of mankind through the Son whom the Father gave, "that whoever believes in him should not perish but have eternal life" (Jn 3:16), comes close to each of us through this Mother. [RH n. 22]

7. MARY'S LOVING AND URGENT INVITATION

Mary Most Holy, the highly favored daughter of the Father, [appears] before the eyes of believers as the perfect model of love towards both God and neighbor. As she herself says in the Canticle of the *Magnificat*, great things were done for her by the Almighty, whose name is holy (see Luke 1:49). The Father chose her for a unique mission in the history of salvation: that of being the Mother of the long-awaited Savior.

The Virgin responded to God's call with complete openness: "Behold, I am the handmaid of the Lord" (Lk 1:38, RSV). Her motherhood, which began in Nazareth and was lived most intensely in Jerusalem at the foot of the Cross, will be felt during this year [of preparation] as a loving and urgent invitation addressed to all the children of God, so that they will return to the house of the Father when they hear her maternal voice: "Do whatever Christ tells you" (see John 2:5). [TMA n. 54]

SIN, CONVERSION, PENANCE, AND MERCY

The journey home to God the Father is a journey of conversion from sin to holiness, from brokenness to wholeness, that travels along the way of repentance.

8. ACKNOWLEDGING OUR SIN

In spite of all the witness of creation... the spirit of darkness (see Ephesians 6:12, Luke 22:53) is capable of showing God as an enemy of His own creature, and in the first place as an enemy of man, as a source of danger and threat to man. In this way Satan manages to sow in man's soul the seed of opposition to the One who from the beginning would be considered as man's enemy—and not as Father. Man is challenged to become the adversary of God!

The analysis of sin in its original dimension indicates that, through the influence of the "father of lies," throughout the history of humanity there will be a constant pressure on man to reject God, even to the point of hating him: "Love of self to the point of contempt for God," as St. Augustine puts it.[2] Man will be inclined to see in God primarily a limitation of himself, and not the source of his own freedom and the fullness of good. [DV n. 38]

In the words of St. John the apostle, "If we say we have no sin, we deceive ourselves, and the truth is not in us. If we confess our sins, he is faithful and just, and will forgive our sins" (1 Jn 1:8-9, RSV). Written at the very dawn of the Church, these inspired words introduce better than any other human expression the theme of sin....

These words present the question of sin in its human dimension: sin as an integral part of the truth about man. But they immediately relate the human dimension to its divine dimension, where sin is countered by the truth of divine love, which is just, generous, and faithful, and which reveals itself above

147

all in forgiveness and redemption. Thus St. John also writes a little further on that "whatever accusations [our conscience] may raise against us, God is greater than our conscience" (see 1 John 3:20).

To acknowledge one's sin, indeed... to recognize oneself as being a sinner, capable of sin and inclined to commit sin, is the essential first step in returning to God. For example, this is the experience of David, who "having done what is evil in the eyes of the Lord" and having been rebuked by the prophet Nathan (see 2 Samuel 11-12), exclaims: "For I know my transgressions, and my sin is ever before me. Against you, you alone, have I sinned and done what is evil in your sight" (see Psalms 51:5-6). Similarly, Jesus Himself puts the following significant words on the lips and in the heart of the prodigal son: "Father, I have sinned against heaven and before you" (Lk 15:18, 21).

In effect, to become reconciled with God presupposes and includes detaching oneself consciously and with determination from the sin into which one has fallen. It presupposes and includes, therefore, doing penance in the fullest sense of the term: repenting, showing this repentance, adopting a real attitude of repentance—which is the attitude of the person who starts out on the road of return to the Father. This is a general law and one which each individual must follow in his or her particular situation. For it is not possible to deal with sin and conversion only in abstract terms. [RP n. 13]

9. SIN, A WOUNDING OF THE CHURCH

Sin is... a wound inflicted upon the Church. In fact, every sin harms the holiness of the ecclesial community. Since all the faithful are in solidarity in the Christian community, there can never be a sin which does not have an effect on the whole community. If it is true that the good done by one person is a benefit and help to all the others, unfortunately it is equally true that the evil committed by one obstructs the perfection to which all are tending....

Reconciliation with God is also reconciliation with the Church, and in a certain sense with all of creation, whose harmony is violated by sin. The Church is the mediatrix of this reconciliation. It is a role assigned to her by her Founder, who gave her the mission and power of forgiving sins. Every instance of reconciliation with God thus takes place in an explicit or implicit, conscious or unconscious, relationship with the Church. [TPS 37/5, 1992, 305]

10. A PROPER SENSE OF SIN

The forgiveness of sins first experienced in baptism is a recurring need in the life of every Christian. Restoring a proper sense of sin is the first step to be taken in facing squarely the grave spiritual crisis looming over men and women today, a crisis which can well be described as "an eclipse of conscience."[3] Without a healthy awareness of their own sinfulness, people will never experience the depth of God's redeeming love for them while they were still sinners (see Romans 5:8). Given the prevailing idea that happiness consists in satisfying oneself and being satisfied with oneself, the Church must proclaim even more vigorously that it is only God's grace, not therapeutic or self-convincing schemes, which can heal the divisions in the human heart caused by sinfulness (see Romans 3:24; Ephesians 2:5). [TPS 38/6, 1993, 371]

11. THE TWOFOLD INJURY OF SIN
As a rupture with God, sin is an act of disobedience by a creature who rejects, at least implicitly, the very One from whom he came and who sustains him in life. It is therefore a suicidal act. Since by sinning man refuses to submit to God, his internal balance is also destroyed and it is precisely within himself that contradictions and conflicts arise.

Wounded in this way, man almost inevitably causes damage to the fabric of his relationship with others and with the created world. This is an objective law and an objective reality, verified in so many ways in the human psyche and in the spiritual life as well as in society, where it is easy to see the signs and effects of internal disorder.

The mystery of sin is composed of this twofold wound which the sinner opens in himself and in his relationship with his neighbor. Therefore one can speak of personal and social sin: from one point of view, every sin is personal; from another point of view, every sin is social insofar as and because it also has social repercussions....

Sin, in the proper sense, is always a personal act, since it is an act of freedom on the part of an individual person and not properly of a group or community. This individual may be conditioned, incited, and influenced by numerous and powerful external factors. He may also be subjected to tendencies, defects, and habits linked with his personal condition. In not a few cases such external and internal factors may attenuate, to a greater or lesser degree, the person's freedom and therefore his responsibility and guilt.

But it is a truth of faith, also confirmed by our experience and reason, that the human person is free. This truth cannot be disregarded in order to place the blame for individuals' sins on external factors such as structures, systems, or other people. Above all, this would be to deny the person's dignity and freedom, which are manifested—even though in a negative and disastrous way—also in this responsibility for sin committed. Hence there is nothing so personal and untransferable in each individual as merit for virtue or responsibility for sin. [RP n. 15, 16]

THE WEEK OF MARCH 21, 1999

12. THE HUMAN CONSCIENCE

Like all things human, even [the] conscience can fail and encounter illusions and errors. It is a delicate voice that can be overpowered by a noisy, distracted way of life, or almost suffocated by a long-lasting and serious habit of sin.

Conscience needs to be nurtured and educated, and the preferred way to form it—at least for those who have the grace of faith—is to relate it to the biblical revelation of the moral law, authoritatively interpreted, with the help of the Holy Spirit, by the Magisterium of the Church. [TPS 39/3, 1993, 166]

The guarantee that objective truth exists is found in God, who is absolute Truth; objectively speaking, the search for truth and the search for God are one and the same.... Every individual has the grave duty to form his or her own conscience in the light of that objective truth which everyone can come to know, and which no one may be prevented from knowing. To claim that one has a right to act according to conscience—but without at the same time acknowledging the duty to conform one's conscience to the truth and to the law which God Himself has written on our hearts—in the end means nothing more than imposing one's limited personal opinion....

On the contrary, the truth must be passionately pursued and lived to the best of one's ability.... Freedom of conscience, rightly understood, is by its very nature always ordered to the truth....

Faced with the obligation of following their own consciences in the search for the truth, the disciples of Jesus Christ know that they may not trust only in their personal capacity for moral discernment. Revelation enlightens their consciences and enables them to know that freedom which is God's great gift to mankind. Not only has He inscribed the natural law within the heart of each individual, in that "most secret core and sanctuary of a man [where] he is alone with God,"[4] but He has also revealed His own law in the Scriptures. Here we find the call, or rather the command, to love God and to observe His law....

More than anyone else, the Christian ought to feel the obligation to conform his conscience to the truth. Before the splendor of the free gift of God's revelation in Christ, how humbly and attentively must he listen to the voice of conscience! How modest must he be in regard to his own limited insight! How quick must he be to learn and how slow to condemn! One of the constant temptations in every age, even among Christians, is to make oneself the norm of truth. In an age of pervasive individualism, this temptation takes a variety of forms. But the mark of those who are in the truth is the ability to love humbly. This is what God's Word teaches us: Truth is expressed in love (see Ephesians 4:15). [TPS 36/4, 1991, 209-210, 212, 215]

THE WEEK OF MARCH 28, 1999

13. ARE WE REPENTANT OR SELF-SATISFIED?

We should take to heart the message of the Gospel parable of the Pharisee and the tax collector (see Luke 18:9-14). The tax collector might possibly have had some justification for the sins he committed, such as to diminish his responsibility. [Yet] his prayer does not dwell on such justifications, but rather on his own unworthiness before God's infinite holiness: "God, be merciful to me a sinner!" (Lk 18:13). The Pharisee, on the other hand, is self-justified, finding some excuse for each of his failings.

Here we encounter two different attitudes of the moral conscience of man in every age. The tax collector represents a repentant conscience, fully aware of the frailty of its own nature and seeing in its own failings, whatever their subjective justifications, a confirmation of its need for redemption. The Pharisee represents a self-satisfied conscience, under the illusion that it is able to observe the law without the help of grace and convinced that it does not need mercy.

All people must take great care not to allow themselves to be tainted by the attitude of the Pharisee,
which would seek to eliminate awareness of one's
own limits and of one's own sin. In our own day this
attitude is expressed particularly in the attempt to
adapt the moral norm to one's own capacities and
personal interests, and even in the rejection of the
very idea of a norm. [VS n. 104-105]

THE WEEK OF APRIL 4, 1999

14. MARY, THE MODEL OF THE MORAL LIFE
Mary is the radiant sign and inviting model of the
moral life.... Mary shares our human condition, but
in complete openness to the grace of God. Not having known sin, she is able to have compassion on
every kind of weakness. She understands sinful man
and loves him with a mother's love.

Precisely for this reason she is on the side of truth
and shares the Church's burden in recalling always
and to everyone the demands of morality. Nor does
she permit sinful man to be deceived by those who
claim to love Him by justifying his sin, for she knows
that the sacrifice of Christ her Son would thus be
emptied of its power. No absolution offered by
beguiling doctrines... can make man truly happy.
Only the Cross and the glory of the risen Christ can
grant peace to his conscience and salvation to his
life. [VS n. 120]

THE WEEK OF APRIL 11, 1999

15. CONVERSION AND PENANCE
In this third year [of preparation] the sense of being
on a journey to the Father should encourage everyone to undertake, by holding fast to Christ the

Redeemer of man, a journey of authentic conversion. This includes both a negative aspect, that of liberation from sin, and a positive aspect, that of choosing good, accepting the ethical values expressed in the natural law, which is confirmed and deepened by the Gospel.

This is the proper context for a renewed appreciation and more intense celebration of the Sacrament of Penance in its most profound meaning. The call to conversion as the indispensable condition of Christian love is particularly important in contemporary society, where the very foundations of an ethically correct vision of human existence often seem to have been lost. [TMA n. 50]

Contemporary man seems to find it harder than ever to recognize his own mistakes and to decide to retrace his steps and begin again after changing course. He seems very reluctant to say "I repent" or "I am sorry." He seems to refuse instinctively and often irresistibly anything that is penance in the sense of a sacrifice accepted and carried out for the correction of sin.

In this regard I would like to emphasize that the Church's penitential discipline, even though it has been mitigated for some time, cannot be abandoned without grave harm both to the interior life of individual Christians and of the ecclesial community and also to their capacity for missionary influence. It is not uncommon for non-Christians to be surprised at the negligible witness of true penance on the part of Christ's followers. It is clear, however, that Christian penance will only be authentic if it is inspired by love and not by mere fear; if it consists in a serious effort to crucify the "old man" so that the "new" can be born by the power of Christ; if it takes as its model Christ, who though He was innocent chose the path of poverty, patience, austerity, and, one can say, the penitential life. [RP n. 26]

Recourse to the Sacrament [of Penance] is necessary when even only one mortal sin has been committed. However, the Christian who believes in the effectiveness of sacramental forgiveness has recourse to the Sacrament with a certain frequency, even when it is not a case of necessity. In it he finds the path for an increasing sensitivity of conscience and an ever-deeper purification, a source of peace, a help in resisting temptation and in striving for a life that responds more and more to the demands of the law and love of God. [TPS 37/5, 1992, p. 306]

THE WEEK OF APRIL 18, 1999

16. THE INDIVIDUAL ASPECT OF PENANCE

In the last years much has been done to highlight in the Church's practice—in conformity with the most ancient tradition of the Church—the community aspect of penance and especially of the Sacrament of Penance. We cannot, however, forget that conversion is a particularly profound inward act in which the individual cannot be replaced by others and cannot make the community be a substitute for him. Although the participation by the fraternal community of the faithful in the penitential celebration is a great help for the act of personal conversion, nevertheless, in the final analysis, it is necessary that in this act there should be a pronouncement by the individual himself with the whole depth of his conscience and with the whole of his sense of guilt and of trust in God, placing himself like the psalmist before God to confess: "Against you... have I sinned" (see Psalms 51:6).

In faithfully observing the centuries-old practice of the Sacrament of Penance—the practice of individual confession with a personal act of sorrow and the intention to amend and make satisfaction—the Church is therefore defending the human soul's individual right. [It is] man's right to a more personal encounter with the crucified forgiving Christ, with Christ saying, through the minister of the Sacrament of Reconciliation: "Your sins are forgiven" (see Mark 2:5); "Go, and do not sin again" (see John 8:11).

As is evident, this is also a right on Christ's part with regard to every human being redeemed by Him. [It is] His right to meet each one of us in that key moment in the soul's life constituted by the moment of conversion and forgiveness. By guarding the Sacrament of Penance, the Church expressly affirms her faith in the mystery of the Redemption as a living and life-giving reality that fits in with man's inward truth, with human guilt and also with the desires of the human conscience.

"Blessed are those who hunger and thirst for righteousness, for they shall be satisfied" (see Matthew 5:6). The Sacrament of Penance is the means to satisfy man with the righteousness that comes from the Redeemer Himself. [RH n. 20]

THE WEEK OF APRIL 25, 1999

17. PENANCE, CHANNEL OF REDEMPTIVE POWER

For a Christian the Sacrament of Penance is the ordinary way of obtaining forgiveness and the remission of serious sin committed after Baptism. Certainly the

Savior and His [saving] action are not so bound to a sacramental sign as to be unable in any period or area of the history of salvation to work outside and above the sacraments. But in the school of faith we learn that the same Savior desired and provided that the simple and precious sacraments of faith would ordinarily be the effective means through which His redemptive power passes and operates.

It would therefore be foolish, as well as presumptuous, to wish arbitrarily to disregard the means of grace and salvation which the Lord has provided and, in the specific case, to claim to receive forgiveness while doing without the Sacrament which was instituted by Christ precisely for forgiveness. The renewal of the rites carried out after the [Second Vatican] Council does not sanction any illusion or alteration in this direction. According to the Church's intention, it was and is meant to stir up in each one of us a new impulse toward the renewal of our interior attitude; toward a deeper understanding of the nature of the Sacrament of Penance; toward a reception of the Sacrament which is more filled with faith, not anxious but trusting; toward a more frequent celebration of the Sacrament which is seen to be completely filled with the Lord's merciful love.... [For] every confessional is a special and blessed place from which, with divisions wiped away, there is born new and uncontaminated a reconciled individual—a reconciled world! [RP n. 31]

18. THE TRIUMPH OF MERCY

Jesus Christ was sent by the Father as the revelation of God's mercy (see John 3:16-18). Christ came not to condemn but to forgive, to show mercy (see Matthew 9:13). And the greatest mercy of all is found in His being in our midst and calling us to meet Him and to confess with Peter that He is "the Son of the living God" (Mt 16:16).

No human sin can erase the mercy of God, or prevent Him from unleashing all His triumphant power, if we only call upon Him. Indeed, sin itself makes even more radiant the love of the Father who, in order to ransom a slave, sacrificed His Son: His mercy toward us is redemption. This mercy reaches its fullness in the gift of the Spirit who bestows new life and demands that it be lived.

No matter how many and great the obstacles put in His way by human frailty and sin, the Spirit, who renews the face of the earth (see Psalms 104:30), makes possible the miracle of the perfect accomplishment of the good. This renewal, which gives the ability to do what is good, noble, beautiful, pleasing to God, and in conformity with His will, is in some way the flowering of the gift of mercy, which offers liberation from the slavery of evil and gives the strength to sin no more. Through the gift of new life, Jesus makes us sharers in His love and leads us to the Father in the Spirit. [VS n. 118]

CHRISTIAN MORAL RESPONSIBILITY
Once we have begun to deal with the roots and results of our personal sin, we are better able to identify our moral respon-sibilities in the wider world.

19. THE CHURCH MUST ACKNOWLEDGE PAST SINS

It is appropriate that, as the second millennium of Christianity draws to a close, the Church should become more fully conscious of the sinfulness of her children, recalling all those times in history when they departed from the spirit of Christ and His Gospel and, instead of offering to the world the witness of a life inspired by the values of faith, indulged in ways of thinking and acting that were truly forms of counterwitness and scandal.

Although she is holy because of her incorporation into Christ, the Church does not tire of doing penance: before God and man she always acknowledges as her own her sinful sons and daughters....

The Holy Door of the Jubilee of the Year 2000 should be symbolically wider than those of previous Jubilees, because humanity, upon reaching this goal, will leave behind not just a century but a millennium. It is fitting that the Church should make this passage with a clear awareness of what has happened to her during the last ten centuries. She cannot cross the threshold of the new millennium without encouraging her children to purify themselves, through repentance, of past errors and instances of infidelity, inconsistency, and slowness to act. Acknowledging the weaknesses of the past is an act of honesty and courage which helps us to strengthen our faith, which alerts us to face today's temptations and challenges, and prepares us to meet them....

On the threshold of the new millennium

160

Christians need to place themselves humbly before the Lord and examine themselves on the responsibility which they too have for the evils of our day. The present age, in fact, together with much light, also presents not a few shadows.

How can we remain silent, for example, about the religious indifference which causes many people today to live as if God did not exist, or to be content with a vague religiosity, incapable of coming to grips with the question of truth and the requirement of consistency? To this must be added the widespread loss of the transcendent sense of human life, and confusion in the ethical sphere, even about the fundamental values of respect for life and the family.

The sons and daughters of the Church too need to examine themselves in this regard. To what extent have they been shaped by the climate of secularism and ethical relativism? And what responsibility do they bear, in view of the increasing lack of religion, for not having shown the true face of God, by having "failed in their religious, moral, or social life"?[5]

It cannot be denied that, for many Christians, the spiritual life is passing through a time of uncertainty which affects not only their moral life but also their life of prayer and the theological correctness of their faith. Faith, already put to the test by the challenges of our times, is sometimes disoriented by erroneous theological views, the spread of which is abetted by the crisis of obedience [to] the Church's Magisterium.

And with respect to the Church of our time, how can we not lament the lack of discernment, which at times becomes even acquiescence, shown by many

Christians concerning the violation of fundamental human rights by totalitarian regimes? And should we not also regret, among the shadows of our own day, the responsibility shared by so many Christians for grave forms of injustice and exclusion? It must be asked how many Christians really know and put into practice the principles of the Church's social doctrine. [TMA n. 33, 36]

<u>THE WEEK OF MAY 16, 1999</u>

20. CLEAR MORAL TEACHING IS LIBERATING

One of the key pastoral problems facing us is the widespread misunderstanding of the role of conscience, whereby individual conscience and experience are exalted above or against Church teaching. The young men and women of America, and indeed of the whole Western world, who are often victims of educational theories which propose that they "create" their own values and that feeling good about themselves is a primary guiding moral principle, are asking to be led out of this moral confusion.

All those who teach in the name of the Church should fearlessly honor the dignity of the moral conscience as the sanctuary in which the voice of God is heard. But with equal care they should proclaim, in opposition to all subjectivism, that conscience is not a tribunal which creates the good, but must be formed in the light of universal and objective norms of morality. Clear teaching on these matters is also an essential part of the necessary return to the practice of the Sacrament of Penance....

Clear teaching on all such matters is liberating because it presents the true meaning of discipleship: Christ calls His followers to friendship with Him (see

John 15:15). In fact, the personal following of Christ is the essential foundation of Christian morality. The "obedience of faith" (Rom 16:26) is both an intellectual assent to doctrine as well as a life commitment which draws us into evermore perfect union with Christ Himself. The Church must always be careful not to reduce "the word of truth" (see Colossians 1:5) to an abstract code of ethics and morality, or a treatise of rules for good behavior. The preaching of Christian morality, so closely linked to the new evangelization, must not empty the Cross of Christ of its power (see 1 Corinthians 1:17). [TPS 39/2, 1994, 117]

At times, in the discussions about new and complex moral problems, it can seem that Christian morality is in itself too demanding, difficult to understand, and almost impossible to practice. This is untrue, since Christian morality consists, in the simplicity of the Gospel in following Jesus Christ, in abandoning oneself to Him, in letting oneself be transformed by His grace and renewed by His mercy—gifts which come to us in the living communion of His Church.... By the light of the Holy Spirit, the living essence of Christian morality can be understood by everyone, even the least learned, but particularly those who are able to preserve an "undivided heart" (see Psalms 86:11). [VS n. 119]

THE FAMILY

If we are to bring healing to a world so deeply loved by the Father, we cannot neglect to care for the family, the foundation of society.

21. MARRIAGE, SIGN OF CHRIST'S LOVE FOR THE CHURCH

Christ's love is the source and the foundation of the love uniting... spouses. It should be stressed that true conjugal love is meant [here], and not mere spontaneous impulse. Today sexuality is often exalted to the point of obscuring the profound nature of love. Certainly, sexual life too has its own genuine value, which can never be underestimated, but it is a limited value that is an insufficient basis for the marriage union, which by its nature depends on total personal commitment.

Every sound psychology and philosophy of love is in agreement on this point. Christian teaching also emphasizes the qualities of the individuals' unitive love and casts a higher light on it, raising it—by virtue of a sacrament—to the level of grace and of sharing in the divine love of Christ. Along these lines St. Paul says of marriage: "This is a great mystery" (Ephesians 5:32), in reference to Christ and the Church. For the Christian, this theological mystery is at the root of the ethics of marriage, conjugal love, and sexual life itself: "Husbands, love your wives, as Christ loved the Church and gave himself up for her" (Eph 5:25).

Grace and the sacramental bond enable conjugal life, as a sign of and share in the love of Christ the Bridegroom, to be a way of holiness for Christian spouses and at the same time to be an effective incentive for the Church to invigorate the communion of the love that distinguishes her. [TPS 40/1, 1995, 27-28]

22. AN INDISSOLUBLE COMMUNION

It is a fundamental duty of the Church to reaffirm strongly... the doctrine of the indissolubility of marriage. To all those who in our times consider it too difficult or indeed impossible to be bound to one person for the whole of life, and to those caught up in a culture that rejects the indissolubility of marriage and openly mocks the commitment of spouses to fidelity, it is necessary to reconfirm the good news of the definitive nature of that conjugal love that has in Christ its foundation and strength.

Being rooted in the personal and total self-giving of the couple and being required by the good of the children, the indissolubility of marriage finds its ultimate truth in the plan that God has manifested in His Revelation: He wills and He communicates the indissolubility of marriage as a fruit, a sign, and a requirement of the absolutely faithful love that God has for man and that the Lord Jesus has for the Church....

The gift of the Sacrament [of Matrimony] is at the same time a vocation and commandment for the Christian spouses, that they may remain faithful to each other forever, beyond every trial and difficulty, in generous obedience to the holy will of the Lord: "What therefore God has joined together, let not man put asunder" (Mt 19:6).

To bear witness to the inestimable value of the indissolubility and fidelity of marriage is one of the most precious and most urgent tasks of Christian couples in our time.... I praise and encourage those numerous couples who, though encountering no small difficulty, preserve and develop the value of

165

indissolubility. Thus in a humble and courageous manner they perform the role committed to them of being a sign—a small and precious sign, sometimes also subjected to temptation, but always renewed—of the unfailing fidelity with which God and Jesus Christ love each and every human being.

But it is also proper to recognize the value of the witness of those spouses who, even when abandoned by their partner, with the strength of faith and of Christian hope have not entered a new union: These spouses too give an authentic witness to fidelity, of which the world today has a great need. For this reason they must be encouraged and helped by the pastors and the faithful of the Church. [FC n. 20]

23. THE TRIALS OF MARRIAGE CAN BE REDEMPTIVE

We must remember that, since the love of Christ the Bridegroom for the Church is a redemptive love, the love of Christian spouses becomes an active participation in Redemption.

Redemption is tied to the Cross: and this helps us to understand and appreciate the meaning of the trials that the couple's life is certainly not spared, but which in God's plan are meant to reinforce their love and bring greater fruitfulness to their married life. Far from promising his married followers an earthly paradise, Jesus Christ offers them the opportunity and the vocation to make a journey with Him which, through difficulties and suffering, will strengthen their union and lead them to a greater joy, as proven by the experience of so many Christian couples, in our day as well. [TPS 40/1, 1995, 28-29]

24. MARRIAGE AND VIRGINITY OR CELIBACY

Virginity or celibacy for the sake of the Kingdom of God not only does not contradict the dignity of marriage but presupposes it and confirms it. Marriage and virginity or celibacy are two ways of expressing and living the one mystery of the covenant of God with His people. When marriage is not esteemed, neither can consecrated virginity or celibacy exist; when human sexuality is not regarded as a great value given by the Creator, the renunciation of it for the sake of the Kingdom of heaven loses its meaning....

Christian couples.... have the right to expect from celibate persons a good example and a witness of fidelity to their vocation until death. Just as fidelity at times becomes difficult for married people and requires sacrifice, mortification, and self-denial, the same can happen to celibate persons, and their fidelity, even in the trials that may occur, should strengthen the fidelity of married couples.

These reflections on virginity or celibacy can enlighten and help those who, for reasons independent of their own will, have been unable to marry and have then accepted their situation in a spirit of service. [FC n. 16]

25. THE SOVEREIGNTY OF THE FAMILY

A person normally comes into the world within a family, and can be said to owe to the family the very fact of his existing as an individual. When he has no family, the person coming into the world develops an

167

anguished sense of pain and loss, one which will subsequently burden his whole life.

The Church draws near with loving concern to all who experience situations such as these, for she knows well the fundamental role which the family is called upon to play. Furthermore, she knows that a person goes forth from the family in order to realize in a new family unit his particular vocation in life. Even if someone chooses to remain single, the family continues to be, as it were, his existential horizon, that fundamental community in which the whole network of social relations is grounded, from the closest and most immediate to the most distant....

Every effort should be made so that the family will be recognized as the primordial and, in a certain sense, sovereign society. The sovereignty of the family is essential for the good of society. A truly sovereign and spiritually vigorous nation is always made up of strong families who are aware of their vocation and mission in history. [TPS 39/4, 1994, 208, 232]

THE WEEK OF JUNE 27, 1999

26. SPIRITUAL FORMATION IN THE FAMILY

The Christian family, as the "domestic Church,..." makes up a natural and fundamental school for formation in the faith. Father and mother receive from the Sacrament of Matrimony the grace and the ministry of the Christian education of their children before whom they bear witness and to whom they transmit both human and religious values. While learning their first words, children learn also the praise of God, whom they feel is near them as a loving and providential Father. While learning the first acts of love, children also learn to open themselves to others, and through the gift of self receive the sense of living as a human being.

The daily life itself of a truly Christian family makes up the first experience of Church, intended to find confirmation and development in an active and responsible process of the children's introduction into the wider ecclesial community and civil society. The more that Christian spouses and parents grow in the awareness that their "domestic Church" participates in the life and mission of the universal Church, so much the more will their sons and daughters be able to be formed in a sense of the Church and will perceive all the beauty of dedicating their energies to the service of the Kingdom of God. [CL n. 62]

The family's catechetical activity has a special character, which is in a sense irreplaceable.... Education in the faith by parents, which should begin from the children's tenderest age, is already being given when the members of a family help each other to grow in faith through the witness of their Christian lives, a witness that is often without words but which perseveres throughout a day-to-day life lived in accordance with the Gospel. This catechesis is more incisive when, in the course of family events (such as the reception of the sacraments, the celebration of the great liturgical feasts, the birth of a child, a bereavement) care is taken to explain in the home the Christian or religious content of these events.

But that is not enough: Christian parents must strive to follow and repeat, within the setting of family life, the more methodical teaching received elsewhere. The fact that these truths about the main questions of faith and Christian living are thus repeated within a family setting impregnated with love and respect will often make it possible to influence the children in a decisive way for life. The parents themselves profit from the effort that this demands of them, for in a catechetical dialogue of this sort each individual both receives and gives.

Family catechesis therefore precedes, accompanies, and enriches all other forms of catechesis. Furthermore, in places where antireligious legislation endeavors even to prevent education in the faith, and in places where widespread unbelief or invasive secularism makes real religious growth practically impossible, "the church of the home"[6] remains the one place where children and young people can receive an authentic catechesis. Thus there cannot be too great an effort on the part of Christian parents to prepare for this ministry of being their own children's catechists and to carry it out with tireless zeal. [CT n. 68]

THE WEEK OF JULY 4, 1999

27. FAMILY PRAYER

Family prayer has its own characteristic qualities. It is prayer offered in common, husband and wife together, parents and children together. Communion in prayer is both a consequence of and a requirement for the communion bestowed by the Sacraments of Baptism and Matrimony. The words with which the Lord Jesus promises His presence can be applied to the members of the Christian family in a special way: "Again I say to you, if two of you agree on earth about anything they ask, it will be done for them by my Father in heaven. For where two or three are gathered in my name, there am I in the midst of them" (Mt 18:19-20].

Family prayer has for its very own object family life itself, which in all its varying circumstances is seen as a call from God and lived as a filial response to His call. Joys and sorrows, hopes and disappointments, births and birthday celebrations, wedding anniversaries of the parents, departures, separations and homecomings, important and far-reaching decisions, the death of those who are dear... all of these mark God's loving intervention in the family's history. They should be seen as suitable moments for thanksgiving, for petition, for trusting abandonment of the family into the hands of their common Father in heaven. The dignity and responsibility of the Christian family as the domestic Church can be achieved only with God's unceasing aid, which will surely be granted if it is humbly and trustingly petitioned in prayer....

By reason of their dignity and mission, Christian parents have the specific responsibility of educating their children in prayer, introducing them to gradual discovery of the mystery of God and to personal dialogue with Him.... The concrete example and living witness of parents is fundamental and irreplaceable in educating their children to pray. Only by praying together with their children can a father and mother—exercising their royal priesthood—penetrate the innermost depths of their children's hearts and leave an impression that the future events in their lives will not be able to efface. [FC n. 59, 60]

28. HONOR WITHIN THE FAMILY

The family is a community of particularly intense interpersonal relationships: between spouses, between parents and children, between generations. It is a community which must be safeguarded in a special way. And God cannot find a better safeguard than this: Honor.

"Honor your father and your mother, that your days may be long in the land which the Lord your God gives to you" (Ex 20:12).... The fourth commandment is closely linked to the commandment of love.... Honor is essentially an attitude of unselfishness. It could be said that it is a sincere gift of person to person, and in that sense honor converges with love.... You parents, the divine precept seems to say, should act in such a way that your life will merit the honor (and the love) of your children! Do not let the divine command that you be honored fall into a moral vacuum! Ultimately then we are speaking of mutual honor.

The commandment "Honor your father and your mother" indirectly tells parents: Honor your sons and your daughters. They deserve this because they are alive, because they are who they are, and this is true from the first moment of their conception. The fourth commandment, then, by expressing the intimate bonds uniting the family, highlights the basis of its inner unity. [TPS 39/4, 1994, 225-6]

29. THE ROLES OF FATHER AND MOTHER

Within the... family... the man is called upon to live his gift and role as husband and father. In his wife he sees the fulfillment of God's intention: "It is not good that the man should be alone; I will make him a helper fit for him" (Gn 2:18), and he makes his own the cry of Adam, the first husband: "This at last is bone of my bones and flesh of my flesh" (Gn 2:23)....

Love for his wife as mother of their children and love for the children themselves are for the man the natural way of understanding and fulfilling his own fatherhood. Above all where social and cultural conditions so easily encourage a father to be less concerned with his family or at any rate less involved in the work of education, efforts must be made to restore socially the conviction that the place and task of the father in and for the family is of unique and irreplaceable importance.

As experience teaches, the absence of a father causes psychological and moral imbalance and notable difficulties in family relationships. [So also] does, in contrary circumstances, the oppressive presence of a father, especially where there still prevails the phenomenon of "machismo," or a wrong superiority of male prerogatives which humiliates women and inhibits the development of healthy family relationships.

In revealing and in reliving on earth the very fatherhood of God, a man is called upon to ensure the harmonious and united development of all the members of the family: He will perform this task by exercising generous responsibility for the life conceived under the heart of the mother; by a more solicitous commitment to education, a task he shares with his wife; by work which is never a cause of division in the family but promotes its unity and stability; and by means of the witness he gives of an adult Christian life which effectively introduces the children into the living experience of Christ and the Church. [FC n. 25]

In rearing children, mothers have a singularly important role. Through the special relationship uniting a mother and her child, particularly in its earliest years of life, she gives the child that sense of security and trust without which the child would find it difficult to develop properly its own personal identity and, subsequently, to establish positive and fruitful relationships with others. This primary relationship between mother and child also has a very particular educational significance in the religious sphere, for it can direct the mind and heart of the child to God long before any formal religious education begins.

In this decisive and sensitive task, no mother should be left alone. Children need the presence and care of both parents, who carry out their duty as educators above all through the influence of the way they live. The quality of the relationship between the spouses has profound psychological effects on children and greatly conditions both the way they relate to their surroundings and the other relationships which they will develop throughout life. [TPS 40/3, 1995, 136-7]

30. THE WORK OF MOTHERS

Experience confirms that there must be a social reevaluation of the mother's role, of the toil connected with it, and of the need that children have for care, love, and affection in order that they may develop into responsible, morally and religiously mature, and psychologically stable persons. It will redound to the credit of society to make it possible for a mother—without inhibiting her freedom, without psychological or practical discrimination, and without penalizing her as compared with other women—to devote herself to taking care of her children and educating them in accordance with their needs, which vary with age. Having to abandon these tasks in order to take up paid work outside the home is wrong from the point of view of the good of society and of the family when it contradicts or hinders these primary goals of the mission of a mother....

The true advancement of women requires that labor should be structured in such a way that women do not have to pay for their advancement by abandoning what is specific to them and at the expense of the family, in which women as mothers have an irreplaceable role. [LE n. 19]

THE WEEK OF AUGUST 1, 1999

31. THE ROLE OF CHILDREN

According to the plan of God, marriage is the foundation of the wider community of the family, since the very institution of marriage and conjugal love is ordained to the procreation and education of children, in whom it finds its crowning.

In its most profound reality, love is essentially a gift; and conjugal love, while leading the spouses to the reciprocal "knowledge" which makes them "one flesh" (Gn 2:24), does not end with the couple, because it makes them capable of the greatest possible gift, the gift by which they become cooperators with God for giving life to a new human person. Thus the couple, while giving themselves to one another, give not just themselves but also the reality of children, who are a living reflection of their love, a permanent sign of conjugal unity and a living and inseparable synthesis of their being a father and a mother.

When they become parents, spouses receive from God the gift of a new responsibility. Their parental love is called to become for the children the visible sign of the very love of God, "from whom every family in heaven and on earth is named" (Eph 3:15). [FC n. 14]

Children are certainly the object of the Lord Jesus' tender and generous love. To them He gave His blessing, and even more, to them He promised the Kingdom of heaven (see Matthew 19:13-15; Mark 10:14). In particular, Jesus exalted the active role that little ones have in the Kingdom of God.

They are the eloquent symbol and exalted image of those moral and spiritual conditions that are essential for entering into the Kingdom of God and for living the logic of total confidence in the Lord: "Truly, I say to you, unless you turn and become like children, you will never enter the kingdom of heaven. Whoever humbles himself like this child, he is the greatest in the kingdom of heaven" (Mt 18:3-5; see also Luke 9:48).

Children are a continual reminder that the missionary fruitfulness of the Church has its life-giving basis not in human means and merits, but in the absolute gratuitous gift of God. The life itself of innocence and grace of many children, and even the suffering and oppression unjustly inflicted upon them, are in virtue of the Cross of Christ a source of spiritual enrichment for them and for the entire Church. [CL n. 47]

32. YOUTH NEED A HIGH MORAL VISION

The well-being of the world's children and young people must be of immense concern to all who have public responsibilities. In my pastoral visits to the Church in every part of the world I have been deeply moved by the almost universal conditions of difficulty in which young people grow up and live. Too many sufferings are visited upon them by natural calamities, famines, epidemics, by economic and political crises, by the atrocities of war....

Where material conditions are at least adequate, other obstacles arise, not the least of which is the breakdown of family values and stability. In developed countries, a serious moral crisis is already affecting the lives of many young people, leaving them adrift, often without hope, and conditioned to look only for immediate gratification.

Yet everywhere there are young men and women deeply concerned about the world around them, ready to give the best of themselves in service to others and particularly sensitive to life's transcendent meaning. But how do we help them? Only by instilling a high moral vision can a society ensure that its young people are given the possibility to mature as free and intelligent human beings, endowed with a

177

robust sense of responsibility to the common good, capable of working with others to create a community and a nation with a strong moral fiber.

America was built on such a vision, and the American people possess the intelligence and will to meet the challenge of rededicating themselves with renewed vigor to fostering the truths on which this country was founded and by which it grew. Those truths are enshrined in the Declaration of Independence, the Constitution, and the Bill of Rights, and they still today receive a broad consensus among Americans. Those truths sustain values which have led people all over the world to look to America with hope and respect.

To all Americans, without exception, I present this invitation: Let us pause and reason together (see Isaiah 1:18). To educate without a value system based on truth is to abandon young people to moral confusion, personal insecurity, and easy manipulation. No country, not even the most powerful, can endure if it deprives its own children of this essential good. Respect for the dignity and worth of every person, integrity and responsibility, as well as understanding, compassion, and solidarity toward others, survive only if they are passed on in families, in schools, and through the communications media. [PS 39/2, 1994, 85-86]

THE WEEK OF AUGUST 15, 1999

33. THE SPECIAL ROLE OF OLDER PEOPLE

Older people [are] oftentimes unjustly considered as unproductive if not directly an insupportable burden. I remind older people that the Church calls and expects them to continue to exercise their mission in the apostolic and missionary life. This is not only a possibility for them, but it is their duty even in this time in their life when age itself provides opportunities in some specific and basic way.

The Bible delights in presenting the older person as the symbol of someone rich in wisdom and fear of the Lord (see Sirach 25:4-6). In this sense the gift of older people can be specifically that of being witness to tradition in the faith, both in the Church and in society (see Psalms 44:2; Exodus 12:26-27), the teacher of the lessons of life (see Sirach 6:34, 8:11-12), and the worker of charity.

At this moment the growing number of older people in different countries worldwide and the expected retirement of persons from various professions and the workplace provides older people with a new opportunity in the apostolate. Involved in the task is their determination to overcome the temptation of taking refuge in a nostalgia—in a never-to-return past—or fleeing from present responsibility because of difficulties encountered in a world of one novelty after another. They must always have a clear knowledge that one's role in the Church and society does not stop at a certain age at all, but at such times knows only new ways of application. As the psalmist says: "They still bring forth fruit in old age, they are ever full of sap and green, to show that the Lord is upright" (see Psalms 92:14-16).... [CL n. 48]

We should remember, as old people, that with health problems and the decline of our physical strength, we are particularly associated with Christ in His Passion and on the Cross. It is therefore possible to penetrate evermore deeply into this mystery of the redeeming sacrifice and to give the witness of faith in this mystery, of the courage and hope that derive from it in the various difficulties and trials of old age.

Everything in the life of the elderly person may serve to fulfill his earthly mission. Nothing is in vain. On the contrary, his cooperation, precisely because it is hidden, is yet more valuable for the Church. [TPS 40/1, 1995, 39]

WOMEN

As the dawn of the third millennium approaches, throughout the world the aspirations of many women once silenced are at last being heard—hopes for justice, for peace, and for an affirmation of the dignity of womanhood. In reflecting on God's love for humanity, we hear His own desire for these aspirations to be realized.

THE WEEK OF AUGUST 22, 1999

34. THE CHURCH IS GRATEFUL FOR WOMEN

The Church gives thanks for each and every woman: for mothers, for sisters, for wives; for women consecrated to God in virginity; for women dedicated to the many human beings who await the gratuitous love of another person; for women who watch over the human persons in the family, which is the fundamental sign of the human community; for women who work professionally, and who at times are burdened by a great social responsibility; for "perfect" women and for "weak" women—for all women as they have come forth from the heart of God in all the beauty and richness of their femininity; as they have been embraced by His eternal love; as, together with men, they are pilgrims on this earth, which is the temporal "homeland" of all people and is transformed sometimes into a "valley of tears"; as they assume, together with men, a common responsibility for the destiny of humanity according to daily necessities and according to that definitive destiny which the human family has in God Himself, in the bosom of the ineffable Trinity.

The Church gives thanks for all the manifestations of the feminine genius which have appeared in the course of history, in the midst of all peoples and nations. She gives thanks for all the charisms which the Holy Spirit distributes to women in the history of the People of God, for all the victories which she owes to their faith, hope, and charity. She gives thanks for all the fruits of feminine holiness.

The Church asks at the same time that these invaluable manifestations of the Spirit (see 1 Corinthians 12:4ff), which with great generosity are poured forth upon the daughters of the eternal Jerusalem, may be attentively recognized and appreciated so that they may return for the common good of the Church and of humanity, especially in our times. Meditating on the biblical mystery of the woman, the Church prays that in this mystery all women may discover themselves and their supreme vocation. [MD n. 31]

35. ADVANCING THE DIGNITY OF WOMEN

If anyone has [the] task of advancing the dignity of women in the Church and society, it is women themselves who must recognize their responsibility as leading characters. There is still much effort to be done in many parts of the world and in various surroundings to destroy that unjust and deleterious mentality which considers the human being as a thing, as an object to buy and sell, as an instrument for selfish interests or for pleasure only. Women themselves, for the most part, are the prime victims of such a mentality. Only through openly acknowledging the personal dignity of women is the first step taken to promote the full participation of women in Church life as well as in social and public life....

The awareness that women with their own gifts and tasks have their own specific vocation has increased and been deepened in the years following the [Second Vatican] Council and has found its fundamental inspiration in the Gospel and the Church's history. In fact, for the believer, the Gospel—namely, the word and example of Jesus Christ—remains the necessary and decisive point of reference. In no other moment in history is this fact more fruitful and innovative.

Though not called to the apostolate of the Twelve, and thereby to the ministerial priesthood, many women nevertheless accompanied Jesus in His ministry and assisted the group of Apostles (see Luke 8:2-3); were present at the foot of the Cross (see Luke 23:49); assisted at the burial of Christ (see Luke 23:55); received and transmitted the message of Resurrection on Easter morn (see Luke 24:1-10); and prayed with the Apostles in the Cenacle awaiting Pentecost (see Acts 1:14).

From the evidence of the Gospel, the Church at

its origin detached herself from the culture of the time and called women to tasks connected with spreading the Gospel. In his letters the Apostle Paul even cites by name a great number of women for their various functions in service of the primitive Christian community (see Romans 16:1-5; Philippians 4:2-3; Colossians 4:15; 1 Corinthians 11:5; 1 Timothy 5:16). "If the witness of the Apostles founds the Church," stated Paul VI, "the witness of women contributes greatly towards nourishing the faith of Christian communities."[7]

Both in her earliest days and in her successive development, the Church, albeit in different ways and with diverse emphases, has always known women who have exercised an oftentimes decisive role in the Church herself and accomplished tasks of considerable value on her behalf. History is marked by grand works, quite often lowly and hidden, but not for this reason any less decisive to the growth and the holiness of the Church. It is necessary that this history continue, indeed that it be expanded and intensified in the face of the growing and widespread awareness of the personal dignity of woman and her vocation, particularly in light of the urgency of a reevangelization and a major effort toward humanizing social relations. [CL n. 49]

THE WEEK OF SEPTEMBER 5, 1999

36. SPECIAL TASKS ENTRUSTED TO WOMEN

Two great tasks entrusted to women merit the attention of everyone. First of all, the task of bringing full dignity to the conjugal life and to motherhood. Today new possibilities are opened to women for a deeper understanding and a richer realization of human and Christian values implied in the conjugal life and the experience of motherhood. Man himself—husband and father—can be helped to overcome forms of absenteeism and of periodic presence as well as a partial fulfillment of parental responsibilities—indeed, he can be involved in new and significant relations of interpersonal communion—precisely as the result of the intelligent, loving, and decisive intervention of woman.

Secondly, women have the task of assuring the moral dimension of culture, the dimension—namely of a culture worthy of the person—of an individual yet social life...."It is not good for man to be alone: let us make him a helper fit for him" (see Genesis 2:18). God entrusted the human being to woman. Certainly, every human being is entrusted to each and every other human being, but in a special way the human being is entrusted to woman, precisely because the woman in virtue of her special experience of motherhood is seen to have a specific sensitivity toward the human person and all that constitutes the individual's true welfare, beginning with the fundamental value of life. How great are the possibilities and responsibilities of woman in this area at a time when the development of science and technology is not always inspired and measured by true wisdom, with the inevitable risk of dehumanizing human life, above all when it would demand a more intense love and a more generous acceptance.

The participation of women in the life of the Church and society in the sharing of her gifts is likewise the path necessary for her personal fulfillment—on which so many justly insist today—and the basic contribution of woman to the enrichment of Church communion and dynamism in the apostolate of the People of God. [CL n. 51]

CHRISTIAN SOCIAL ACTION
To share the heart of the Father is to share His concern for those most in need—in need, not only of material goods, but of healing and reconcilation as well.

THE WEEK OF SEPTEMBER 12, 1999

37. CARING FOR THOSE MOST IN NEED
In the presence of suffering we cannot remain indifferent or passive. Before asking about the responsibility of others, believers listen to the voice of their Divine Master, who urges them to imitate the Good Samaritan, who dismounted in order to help the man who had been attacked by robbers on the road from Jerusalem to Jericho and spent his energy, time, and money for him. First and foremost he offered him his compassionate heart (see Luke 10:30-37). Christians know they are called to put Christ's teaching into practice: "Whatever you did for one of these least brothers of mine, you did for me" (see Matthew 25:40)....

Jesus came to proclaim the Gospel to the poor, to those who, aware of their limitations, feel the need of help from on high. Only the person who is poor in this sense, who is not proud or self-inflated, can understand that the wealth of light and grace received from God calls in turn for a free offering of one's life for others.

For believers this is both an individual and a social duty. The example comes from the primitive Church, which gathered around the Apostles not only to hear their preaching and celebrate the Eucharist but also to exercise charity with them. For this purpose they laid their possessions at the feet of the Apostles so that they could be distributed in turn to the poor. [TPS 38/3, 1993, 170]

The option or love of preference for the poor.... is an option, or a special form of primacy in the exercise of Christian charity, to which the whole tradition of the Church bears witness. It affects the life of each Christian inasmuch as he or she seeks to imitate the life of Christ, but it applies equally to our social responsibilities and hence to our manner of living, and to the logical decisions to be made concerning the ownership and use of goods....

It is necessary to state once more the characteristic principle of Christian social doctrine: the goods of this world are originally meant for all. The right to private property is valid and necessary, but it does not nullify the value of this principle. [SRS n. 42]

As far as the Church is concerned, the social message of the Gospel must not be considered a theory, but above all else a basis and a motivation for action. Inspired by this message, some of the first Christians distributed their goods to the poor, bearing witness to the fact that, despite different social origins, it was possible for people to live together in peace and harmony. Through the power of God, down the centuries monks tilled the land, men and women religious founded hospitals and shelters for the poor, confraternities as well as individual men and women

of all states of life devoted themselves to the needy
and to those on the margins of society—convinced as
they were that Christ's words "As you did it to one of
the least of these my brethren, you did it to me" (Mt
25:40) were not intended to remain a pious wish but
were meant to become a concrete life commitment.
[CA n. 57]

38. NO RECONCILIATION WITHOUT CONVERSION

Sacred Scripture speaks to us of... reconciliation,
inviting us to make every effort to attain it. But
Scripture also tells us that it is above all a merciful
gift of God to humanity. The history of salvation—
the salvation of the whole of humanity as well as of
every human being of whatever period—is the wonderful history of a reconciliation: the reconciliation
whereby God, as Father, in the blood and the Cross
of His Son made man, reconciles the world to
Himself and thus brings into being a new family of
those who have been reconciled.

Reconciliation becomes necessary because there
has been the break of sin from which derive all the
other forms of break within man and about him.
Reconciliation, therefore, in order to be complete
necessarily requires liberation from sin, which is to
be rejected in its deepest roots. Thus a close internal
link unites conversion and reconciliation. It is impossible to split these two realities or to speak of one and
say nothing of the other....

There can be no union among people without an
internal change in each individual. Personal conver-

sion is the necessary path to harmony between individuals. When the Church proclaims the good news of reconciliation or proposes achieving it through the sacraments, she is exercising a truly prophetic role: condemning the evils of man in their infected source; showing the root of divisions; and bringing hope in the possibility of overcoming tensions and conflict and reaching brotherhood, concord, and peace at all levels and in all sections of human society.

She is changing a historical condition of hatred and violence into a civilization of love. She is offering to everyone the evangelical and sacramental principle of that reconciliation at the source, from which comes every other gesture or act of reconciliation, also at the social level. [RP n. 4]

THE SPHERES OF HUMAN LIFE:
POLITICS, ECONOMICS, CULTURE, SCIENCE
To labor for the coming of God's Kingdom is to seek to penetrate every sphere of human endeavor with values that affirm the Father's love for the world.

THE WEEK OF SEPTEMBER 26, 1999
39. CHARITY AND JUSTICE IN PUBLIC LIFE
A charity that loves and serves the person is never able to be separated from justice. Each in its own way demands the full, effective acknowledgement of the rights of the individual to which society is ordered in all its structures and institutions.

In order to achieve their task directed to the Christian animation of the temporal order, in the sense of serving persons and society, the lay faithful are never to relinquish their participation in public life, that is, in the many different economic, social, legislative, administrative, and cultural areas which are intended to promote organically and institutionally the common good.... Every person has a right and duty to participate in public life, albeit in a diversity and complementarity of forms, levels, tasks, and responsibilities. Charges of careerism, idolatry of power, egoism, and corruption that are oftentimes directed at persons in government, parliaments, the ruling classes, or political parties—as well as the common opinion that participating in politics is an absolute moral danger—do not in the least justify either skepticism or an absence on the part of Christians in public life. [CL n. 42]

THE WEEK OF OCTOBER 3, 1999

40. THE CHRISTIAN IN POLITICS

The spirit of service is a fundamental element in the exercise of political power. This spirit of service, together with the necessary competence and efficiency, can make virtuous or above criticism the activity of persons in public life which is justly demanded by the rest of the people. To accomplish this requires a full-scale battle and a determination to overcome every temptation, such as the recourse to disloyalty and to falsehood; the waste of public funds for the advantage of a few and those with special interests; and the use of ambiguous and illicit means for acquiring, maintaining, and increasing power at any cost....

The lay faithful must bear witness to those human

and Gospel values that are intimately connected with political activity itself, such as liberty and justice, solidarity, faithful and unselfish dedication for the good of all, a simple lifestyle, and a preferential love for the poor and the least. This demands that the lay faithful always be more animated by a real participation in the life of the Church and enlightened by her social doctrine. In this they can be supported and helped by the nearness of the Christian community and their pastors. [CL n. 42]

When people think they possess the secret of a perfect social organization which makes evil impossible, they also think that they can use any means, including violence and deceit, in order to bring that organization into being. Politics then becomes a secular religion which operates under the illusion of creating paradise in this world. But no political society—which possesses its own autonomy and laws—can ever be confused with the Kingdom of God.

The Gospel parable of the weeds among the wheat (see Matthew 13:24-30, 36-43) teaches that it is for God alone to separate the subjects of the Kingdom from the subjects of the Evil One, and that this judgment will take place at the end of time. By presuming to anticipate judgment here and now, people put themselves in the place of God and set themselves against the patience of God.

Through Christ's sacrifice on the Cross, the victory of the Kingdom of God has been achieved once and for all. Nevertheless, the Christian life involves a struggle against temptation and the forces of evil. Only at the end of history will the Lord return in glory for the final judgment (see Matthew 25:31) with the establishment of a new heaven and a new earth (see 2 Peter 3:13; Revelation 21:1). But as long as time lasts, the struggle between good and evil continues even in the human heart itself. [CA n. 25]

Authentic democracy is possible only in a State ruled by law and on the basis of a correct conception of the human person. It requires that the necessary conditions be present for the advancement... of the individual through education and formation in true ideals, and... through the creation of structures of participation and shared responsibility.

Nowadays there is a tendency to claim that agnosticism and skeptical relativism are the philosophy and the basic attitude which correspond to democratic forms of political life. Those who are convinced that they know the truth and firmly adhere to it are considered unreliable from a democratic point of view, since they do not accept that truth is determined by the majority, or that it is subject to variation according to different political trends. [But] it must be observed in this regard that if there is no ultimate truth to guide and direct political activity, then ideas and convictions can easily be manipulated for reasons of power. As history demonstrates, a democracy without values easily turns into open or thinly disguised totalitarianism. [CA n. 46]

THE WEEK OF OCTOBER 10, 1999

41. THE CHRISTIAN IN THE WORKPLACE

In the context of the transformations taking place in the world of economy and work which are a cause of concern, the lay faithful have the responsibility of being in the forefront in working out a solution to the very serious problems of growing unemployment; to fight for the most opportune overcoming of numerous injustices that come from organizations of work which lack a proper goal; to make the workplace become a community of persons respected in their uniqueness and in their right to participation; to develop new solidarity among those that participate in a common work; to raise up new forms of business enterprising and to look again at systems of commerce, finance, and exchange of technology. To such an end the lay faithful must accomplish their work with professional competence, with human honesty, with a Christian spirit, and especially as a way of their own sanctification.... [CL n. 43]

The Church acknowledges the legitimate role of profit as an indication that a business is functioning well. When a firm makes a profit, this means that production factors have been properly employed and corresponding human needs have been duly satisfied.

But profitability is not the only indicator of a firm's condition. It is possible for the financial accounts to be in order, and yet for the people—who make up the firm's most valuable asset—to be humiliated and their dignity offended.

Besides being morally inadmissible, this will eventually have negative repercussions on the firm's economic efficiency. In fact, the purpose of a business firm is not simply to make a profit, but is to be found in its very existence as a community of persons who in various ways are endeavoring to satisfy their basic needs, and who form a particular group at the service of the whole of society. Profit is the regulator of the life of a business, but it is not the only one. Other human and moral factors must also be considered which, in the long term, are at least equally important for the life of a business. [CA n. 35]

There are collective and qualitative needs which cannot be satisfied by market mechanisms. There are important human needs which escape its logic. There are goods which by their very nature cannot and must not be bought or sold.

Certainly the mechanisms of the market offer secure advantages: they help to utilize resources better; they promote the exchange of products; above all they give central place to the person's desires and preferences, which, in a contract, meet the desires and preferences of another person. Nevertheless, these mechanisms carry the risk of an idolatry of the market, an existence which ignores the existence of goods which by their nature are not and cannot be mere commodities. [CA n. 40]

THE WEEK OF OCTOBER 17, 1999

42. THE CHRISTIAN IN CULTURE

The Church calls upon the lay faithful to be present as signs of courage and intellectual creativity in the privileged places of culture, that is, the world of education—school and university—in places of scientific and technological research, the areas of artistic creativity and work in the humanities. Such a presence is destined not only for the recognition and possible purification of the elements that critically burden existing culture, but also for the elevation of these cultures through the riches which have their source in the Gospel and the Christian faith. [CL n. 44]

Christian wisdom, which the Church teaches by divine authority, continuously inspires the faithful of Christ zealously to endeavor to relate human affairs and activities with religious values in a single living synthesis. Under the direction of these values all things are mutually connected for the glory of God and the integral development of the human person, a development that includes both corporal and spiritual well-being.

Indeed, the Church's mission of spreading the Gospel not only demands that the Good News be preached ever more widely and to ever-greater numbers of men and women, but that the very power of the Gospel should permeate thought patterns, standards of judgment, and norms of behavior. In a word, it is necessary that the whole of human culture be steeped in the Gospel.

The cultural atmosphere in which a human being lives has a great influence upon his or her way of thinking and, thus, of acting. Therefore, a division between faith and culture is more than a small impediment to evangelization, while a culture penetrated with the Christian spirit is an instrument that favors the spreading of the Good News. [SC n. 5]

THE WEEK OF OCTOBER 24, 1999

43. SCIENCE, FAITH, AND THE WORLD'S FUTURE

"Science and faith are both gifts of God." This terse statement not only excludes the idea that science and faith must view one another with mutual suspicion, but also shows the deepest reason calling them to establish a constructive and cordial relationship:

God, the common foundation of both; God, the ultimate reason for the logic of creation which science
explores, and the source of the Revelation by which
He freely gives Himself to man, calling him to faith,
in order to make him a son instead of a creature,
and opening to him the gates of intimacy with Him.
The light of reason, which makes science possible,
and the light of Revelation, which makes faith possible, emanate from a single source....

The dialogue between science and faith, each
respecting the other's areas, is doubly necessary in
the domain of applied science.... It is at the level of
applied science that humanity experiences, for better or worse, the power of scientific knowledge. If
human life is at enormous risk today, it is not
because of the truth discovered through scientific
research, but because of the deadly applications
made of it on the technological level....

Whenever scientific activity has a positive effect on
respect for and protection of human dignity, it contributes significantly to building peace. Therefore it
is necessary to be tireless in promoting a scientific
culture capable of looking always at the whole person and at the whole of peoples, serving the universal good and solidarity. In this regard, great importance is attached to making progress in the dialogue
between science and faith.

We must work together to reestablish the connection between truth and values, between science and
ethical commitment. We must all be truly convinced
that progress is really such if it is at the service of the
true and total well-being of individuals and of the
whole human family.... Although science's main task

is to seek the truth in the free and legitimate liberty belonging to it, scientists are nevertheless not permitted to prescind from the ethical implications concerning the means of their research and the use of the truths they discover. Ethical goodness is simply another name for truth sought by the practical intellect....

My well-founded hope is that the Church and the scientific community may share their wealth of knowledge and experience in an evermore intense, cordial, and fruitful dialogue so that all creatures may participate in fulfilling God's loving plan.... May... scientists who especially cultivate the intellect also cultivate love. [TPS 38/5, 1993, 296-300]

44. RESPECT FOR CREATION

Today in an ever-increasingly acute way, the... ecological question poses itself.... Certainly humanity has received from God Himself the task of dominating the created world and cultivating the garden of the world. But this is a task that humanity must carry out in respect for the divine image received [in human nature], and therefore with intelligence and with love, assuming responsibility for the gifts that God has bestowed and continues to bestow. Humanity has in its possession a gift that must be passed on to future generations, if possible, passed on in a better condition....

The dominion granted to man by the Creator is not an absolute power, nor can one speak of a freedom to use and misuse, or to dispose of things as one pleases. The limitation imposed from the beginning by the Creator Himself and expressed symbolically by the prohibition not to "eat of the fruit of the tree" (see Genesis 2:16-17) shows clearly enough that, when it comes to the natural world, we are subject not only to biological laws but also to moral ones which cannot be violated with impunity. A true concept of development cannot ignore the use of the things of nature, the renewability of resources and the consequences of haphazard industrialization— three considerations which alert our consciences to the moral dimension of development."[8] [CL n. 43]

WITNESSES TO THE GOSPEL OF LIFE
The gospel of God's love for humanity and the gospel of life are a single and indivisible gospel.

THE WEEK OF NOVEMBER 7, 1999

45. THE WORTH OF THE HUMAN PERSON
Man is called to a fullness of life which far exceeds the dimensions of his earthly existence, because it consists in sharing the very life of God. The loftiness of this supernatural vocation reveals the greatness and the inestimable value of human life even in its temporal phase....

The Church knows that this Gospel of life, which she has received from her Lord, has a profound and persuasive echo in the heart of every person—believer and nonbeliever alike—because it marvelously fulfills all the heart's expectations while infinitely surpassing them. Even in the midst of difficulties and uncertainties, every person sincerely open to truth and goodness can, by the light of reason and the hidden action of grace, come to recognize in the natural law written in the heart (see Romans 2:14-15) the sacred value of human life from its very beginning until its end, and can affirm the right of every human being to have this primary good respected to the highest degree. Upon the recognition of this right, every human community and the political community itself are founded....

Man's life comes from God; it is His gift, His image and imprint, a sharing in His breath of life. God therefore is the sole Lord of this life: man cannot do with it as He wills. God Himself makes this clear to Noah after the Flood: "For your own lifeblood, too, I will demand an accounting... and from man in regard to his fellowman I will demand an accounting for human life" (see Genesis 9:5). The biblical text is concerned to emphasize how the sacredness of life has its foundation in God and in his creative activity: "For God made man in his own image" (Gn 9:6).

Human life and death are thus in the hands of God, in his power: "In his hand is the life of every living thing and the breath of all mankind," exclaims Job (12:10). "The Lord brings to death and brings to life; he brings down to Sheol and raises up" (see 1 Samuel 2:6). He alone can say: "It is I who bring both death and life" (see Deuteronomy 32:39). [EV n. 2, 39]

THE WEEK OF NOVEMBER 14, 1999

46. ABORTION, AN UNSPEAKABLE CRIME

Among all the crimes which can be committed against life, procured abortion has characteristics making it particularly serious and deplorable. The Second Vatican Council defines abortion, together with infanticide, as an "unspeakable crime."[9]

But today, in many people's consciences, the perception of its gravity has become progressively obscured. The acceptance of abortion in the popular mind, in behavior, and even in law itself, is a telling sign of an extremely dangerous crisis of the moral sense, which is becoming more and more incapable of distinguishing between good and evil, even when the fundamental right to life is at stake. Given such a grave situation, we need now more than ever to have the courage to look the truth in the eye and to call things by their proper name, without yielding to convenient compromises or to the temptation of self-deception.

In this regard the reproach of the prophet is extremely straightforward: "Woe to those who call evil good and good evil, who put darkness for light and light for darkness" (Is 5:20). Especially in the case of abortion there is a widespread use of ambiguous terminology, such as "interruption of pregnancy," which tends to hide abortion's true nature and to attenuate its seriousness in public opinion. Perhaps this linguistic phenomenon is itself a symptom of an uneasiness of conscience. But no word has the power to change the reality of things: procured abortion is *the deliberate and direct killing, by whatever means it is carried out, of a human being in the initial phase of his or her existence, extending from conception to birth.*

The moral gravity of procured abortion is apparent in all its truth if we recognize that we are dealing with murder. [EV n. 58]

47. DEFEND LIFE!

America, you are beautiful and blessed in so many ways.... But your best beauty and richest blessing is found in the human person: in each man, woman, and child, in every immigrant, in every native-born son and daughter.... The ultimate test of your greatness is the way you treat every human being, but especially the weakest and most defenseless ones.

The best traditions of your land presume respect for those who cannot defend themselves. If you want equal justice for all, and true freedom and lasting peace, then, America, defend life! All the great causes that are yours today will have meaning only to the extent that you guarantee the right to life and protect the human person. [TPS 39/2, 1994, 86]

INTERRELIGIOUS DIALOGUE

Interreligious dialogue cannot replace the task of evangeliza-tion, but it is part of our demonstration of the Father's love for the people of all nations.

48. PART OF THE CHURCH'S EVANGELIZING MISSION

Interreligious dialogue is a part of the Church's evangelizing mission. Understood as a method and means of mutual knowledge and enrichment, dialogue is not in opposition to the mission *ad gentes* ["to the nations"]; indeed, it has special links to that mission and is one of its expressions. This mission, in fact, is addressed to those who do not know Christ and his Gospel, and who belong for the most part to other religions.

In Christ, God calls all peoples to Himself and He wishes to share with them the fullness of His revelation and love. He does not fail to make Himself present in many ways, not only to individuals but also to entire peoples through their spiritual riches, of which their religions are the main and essential expression, even when they contain "gaps, insufficiencies and errors."[10] All of this has been given ample emphasis by the [Second Vatican] Council and the subsequent Magisterium, without detracting in any way from the fact that salvation comes from Christ and that dialogue does not dispense from evangelization.

In the light of the economy of salvation, the Church sees no conflict between proclaiming Christ and engaging in interreligious dialogue. Instead, she feels the need to link the two in the context of her mission *ad gentes.* These two elements must maintain both their intimate connection and their distinctiveness; therefore they should not be confused, manipulated, or regarded as identical, as though they were interchangeable.

I recently wrote to the bishops of Asia: "Although the Church gladly acknowledges whatever is true and holy in the religious traditions of Buddhism, Hinduism, and Islam as a reflection of that truth which enlightens all people, this does not lessen her duty and resolve to proclaim without fail Jesus Christ who is 'the Way, and the Truth, and the Life....' The fact that the followers of other religions can receive

God's grace and be saved by Christ apart from the ordinary means which He has established does not thereby cancel the call to faith and Baptism which God wills for all people."[11]

Indeed Christ Himself, "while expressly insisting on the need for faith and Baptism, at the same time confirmed the need for the Church, into which people enter through Baptism as through a door." Dialogue should be conducted and implemented with the conviction that the Church is the ordinary means of salvation and that she alone possesses the fullness of the means of salvation. [RM n. 55]

THE WEEK OF DECEMBER 5, 1999

49. DIALOGUE BASED ON RESPECT, HOPE, AND LOVE

[Inter-religious] dialogue does not originate from tactical concerns or self-interest, but is an activity with its own guiding principles, requirements, and dignity. It is demanded by deep respect for everything that has been brought about in human beings by the Spirit who blows where He wills. Through dialogue, the Church seeks to uncover the "seeds of the Word,"[12] a "ray of truth which enlightens all people"[13]; these are found in individuals and in the religious traditions of humanity.

Dialogue is based on hope and love, and will bear fruit in the Spirit. Other religions constitute a positive challenge for the Church: they stimulate her both to discover and acknowledge the signs of Christ's presence and the working of the Spirit, as well as to examine more deeply her own identity and to bear witness to the fullness of Revelation which she has received for the good of all.

This gives rise to the spirit which must enliven dialogue in the context of mission. Those engaged in this dialogue must be consistent with their own religious traditions and convictions, and be open to understanding those of the other party without pretense or close-mindedness, but with truth, humility, and frankness, knowing that dialogue can enrich each side. There must be no abandonment of principles nor false irenicism, but instead a witness given and received for mutual advancement on the road of religious inquiry and experience, and at the same time for the elimination of prejudice, intolerance, and misunderstandings. Dialogue leads to inner purification and conversion which, if pursued with docility to the Holy Spirit, will be spiritually fruitful. [RM n. 56]

WORKING FOR PEACE

"Blessed are the peacemakers," Jesus said; they have the high honor of being known as children of God, because they are fulfilling the desire of their heavenly Father (Mt 5:9).

THE WEEK OF DECEMBER 12, 1999

50. BUILDING PEACE

Precisely because of their faith, believers are called—as individuals and as a body—to be messengers and artisans of peace. Like others and even more than others, they are called to seek with humility and perseverance appropriate responses to the yearnings for security and freedom, solidarity and sharing, which are common to everyone in this world, which as it were has become smaller. A commitment to peace of course concerns every person of good will.... Yet this is a duty which is especially incumbent upon all who profess faith in God and even more so upon Christians, who have as their guide and master the "Prince of Peace" (Is 9:6)....

"Peace I leave with you; my peace I give to you," Christ has said to us (Jn 14:27). This divine promise fills us with the hope, indeed the certainty of divine hope, that peace is possible, because nothing is impossible with God (see Luke 1:37). For true peace is always God's gift, and for us Christians it is a precious gift of the risen Lord....

I wish to reaffirm the need for intense, humble, confident, and persevering prayer, if the world is finally to become a dwelling place of peace.

Prayer is *par excellence* the power needed to implore that peace and obtain it. It gives courage and support to all who love this good and desire to promote it in accordance with their own possibilities and in the various situations in which they live. Prayer not only opens us up to a meeting with the Most High but also disposes us to a meeting with our neighbor, helping us to establish with everyone, without discrimination, relationships of respect, understanding, esteem, and love....

Prayer is the bond which most effectively unites us. It is through prayer that believers meet one another at a level where inequalities, misunderstandings, bitterness, and hostility are overcome, namely before God, the Lord and Father of all. Prayer, as the authentic expression of a right relationship with God and with others, is already a positive contribution to peace. [TPS 37/3, 1992, 161-3, 166]

51. PEACE AND JUSTICE

Peace is a fundamental good which involves respecting and promoting essential human values: the right to life at every stage of its development; the right to be respected, regardless of race, sex, or religious convictions; the right to the material goods necessary for life; the right to work and to a fair distribution of its fruits for a well-ordered and harmonious coexistence. As individuals, as believers, and even more as Christians, we must feel the commitment to living these values of justice, which are crowned by the supreme law of love: "You shall love your neighbor as yourself" (Mt 22:39). [TPS 37/3, 1992, 164-5]

52. PEACE IS POSSIBLE

Peace is not a utopia, nor an inaccessible ideal, nor an unrealizable dream.

War is not an inevitable calamity.

Peace is possible.

And because it is possible, peace is our duty: our grave duty, our supreme responsibility.

Certainly peace is difficult; certainly it demands much good will, wisdom, and tenacity. But man can and he must make the force of reason prevail over the reasons of force.... And since peace, entrusted to the responsibility of men and women, remains even then a gift of God, it must also express itself in prayer to Him who holds the destinies of all peoples in His hands. [NE n. 13]

A FINAL WORD ON THE GREAT JUBILEE

I invite the faithful to raise to the Lord fervent prayers to obtain the light and assistance necessary for the preparation and celebration of the forthcoming Jubilee. I exhort my Venerable Brothers in the Episcopate and the ecclesial communities entrusted to them to open their hearts to the promptings of the Spirit. He will not fail to arouse enthusiasm and lead people to celebrate the Jubilee with renewed faith and generous participation.

I entrust this responsibility of the whole Church to the maternal intercession of Mary, Mother of the Redeemer. She, the Mother of Fairest Love, will be for Christians on the way to the Great Jubilee of the third millennium the star which safely guides their steps to the Lord. May the unassuming young woman of Nazareth, who two thousand years ago offered to the world the Incarnate Word, lead the men and women of the new millennium toward the One who is "the true light that enlightens every man" (Jn 1:9). [TMA n. 59]

AS THE THIRD MILLENNIUM DRAWS NEAR

(The complete official text of the apostolic letter Tertio Millennio Adveniente *by His Holiness Pope John Paul II, released on November 14, 1994.)*

To the Bishops, Priests and Deacons, Men and Women Religious, and All the Lay Faithful

INTRODUCTION

1. As the third millennium of the new era draws near, our thoughts turn spontaneously to the words of the Apostle Paul, "When the fullness of time had come, God sent forth his Son, born of woman" (Gal 4:4). *The fullness of time coincides with the mystery of the Incarnation of the Word,* of the Son who is of one being with the Father, and with the mystery of the Redemption of the world. In this passage, St. Paul emphasizes that the Son of God was born of woman, born under the Law, and came into the world in order to redeem all who were under the Law so that they might receive adoption as sons and daughters. And he adds, "Because you are sons, God has sent the Spirit of his Son into our hearts, crying 'Abba! Father!'" His conclusion is truly comforting: "So through God you are no longer a slave but a son, and if a son then an heir" (Gal 4:6-7).

Paul's presentation of the mystery of the Incarnation contains *the Revelation of the mystery of the Trinity and the continuation of the Son's mission in the mission of the Holy Spirit.* The Incarnation of the Son of God, His conception and birth, is the prerequisite for the sending of the Holy Spirit. This text of St. Paul *thus allows the fullness of the mystery of the Redemptive Incarnation to shine forth.*

I
"JESUS CHRIST IS THE SAME YESTERDAY AND TODAY"
(Heb 13:8)

2. In his Gospel Luke has handed down to us a *concise narrative of the circumstances of Jesus' birth:* "In those days a decree went out from Caesar Augustus that all the world should be enrolled.... And all went to be enrolled, each to his own city. And Joseph also went up from Galilee, from the city of Nazareth, to Judea, to the city of David, which is called Bethlehem, because he was of the house and lineage of David, to be enrolled with Mary, his betrothed, who was with child. And while they were there, the time came for her to be delivered. And she gave birth to her first-born son and wrapped him in swaddling cloths, and laid him in a manger, because there was no place for them in the inn" (Lk 2:1, 3-7).

Thus was fulfilled what the Angel Gabriel foretold at the Annunciation, when he spoke to the Virgin of Nazareth in these words: "Hail, full of grace, the Lord is with you" (Lk 1:28). Mary was troubled by these words, and so the divine messenger quickly added: "Do not be afraid, Mary, for you have found favor with God. And behold, you will conceive in your womb and bear a son, and you shall call his name Jesus. He will be great and will be called the Son of the Most High.... The Holy Spirit will come upon you and the power of the Most High will overshadow you; therefore the child to be born will be called holy, the Son of God" (Lk 1:30-32, 35). Mary's reply to the angel was unhesitating: "Behold, I am the handmaid of the Lord; let it be to me according to your word" (Lk 1:38). Never in human history did so much depend, as it did then, upon the consent of one human creature.[1]

3. John, in the Prologue of his Gospel, captures in one phrase all the depth of the mystery of the Incarnation. He writes, *"And the Word became flesh and dwelt among us,* full of grace and truth; we have beheld his glory, glory as of the only Son from the Father"* (1:14, RSV). For John, the Incarnation of the Eternal Word, of one being with the Father, took place in the conception and birth of Jesus. The Evangelist speaks of the Word who in the beginning was with God, and through whom everything which exists was made; the Word in whom was life, the life which was the light of men (cf. 1:1-4). Of the only-begotten Son, God from God, the Apostle Paul writes that He is *"the first-born of all creation"* (Col 1:15). God created the world through the Word. The Word is Eternal Wisdom; the Thought and Substantial Image of God; "He reflects the glory of God and bears the very stamp of his nature" (Heb 1:3). Eternally begotten and eternally loved by the Father, as God from God and Light from Light, he is the principle and archetype of everything created by God in time.

The fact that in the fullness of time the Eternal Word took on the condition of a creature gives a unique *cosmic value* to the event which took place in Bethlehem two thousand years ago. *Thanks to the Word, the world of creatures appears as a "cosmos," an* ordered universe. And it is the same Word who, *by taking flesh, renews the cosmic order of creation.* The Letter to the Ephesians speaks of the purpose which God had set forth in Christ, "as a plan for the fulness of time, *to unite all things in him,* things in heaven and things on earth" (Eph 1:9-10).

4. Christ, the Redeemer of the world, *is the one Mediator between God and men,* and there is no other name under heaven by which we can be saved (cf. Acts 4:12). As we read in the Letter to the Ephesians: "In him we have redemption through his blood, the forgiveness of our trespasses, according to the richness of his grace, which he has lavished upon us. For he has made known to us in all wisdom and insight... his purpose which he set forth in Christ as a plan for the fulness of time, to unite all things in him, things in heaven and things on earth" (1:7-10). Christ, the Son who is of one being with the Father, is therefore the one who *reveals God's plan for all creation, and for man in particular.* In the memorable phrase of the Second Vatican Council, Christ "fully reveals man to man himself and makes his supreme calling clear."[2] He shows us this calling by revealing the mystery of the Father and His love. As the image of the invisible God, Christ is the perfect man who has restored to the children of Adam the divine likeness which had been deformed by sin. In His human nature, free from all sin and assumed into the divine Person of the Word, the nature shared by all human beings is raised to a sublime dignity: "By his incarnation the Son of God *united himself in some sense with every man.* He labored with human hands, thought with a human mind, acted with a human will and loved with a human heart. Born of Mary the Virgin he truly became one of us and, sin apart, was like us in every way."[3]

5. This "becoming one of us" on the part of the Son of God took place in the greatest humility, so it is no wonder that secular historians, caught up by more stirring events and by famous personages, first made only passing, albeit significant, references to Him. Such references to Christ are found for example in *The Antiquities of the Jews,* a work compiled in Rome between the years 93 and 94 by the historian Flavius Josephus,[4] and especially in the *Annals* of Tacitus, written between the years 115 and 120, where, reporting the burning of Rome in the year 64, falsely attributed by Nero to the Christians, the historian makes an explicit reference to Christ "executed by order of the procurator Pontius Pilate during the reign of Tiberius."[5] Suetonius, too, in his biography of the emperor Claudius, written around 121, informs us that the Jews were expelled from Rome because "under the instigation of a certain Chrestus they stirred up frequent riots."[6] This passage is generally interpreted as referring to Jesus Christ, who had become a source of contention within Jewish circles in Rome. Also of importance as proof of the rapid spread of Christianity is the testimony of Pliny the Younger, the Governor of Bithynia, who reported to the Emperor Trajan, between the years 111 and 113, that a large number of people were accustomed to gather "on a designated day, before dawn, to sing in alternating choirs a hymn to Christ as to a God."[7]

But the great event which non-Christian historians

merely mention in passing takes on its full significance in the writings of the New Testament. These writings, although documents of faith, are no less reliable as historical testimonies, if we consider their references as a whole. Christ, true God and true man, the Lord of the cosmos, is also the Lord of history, of which He is "the Alpha and the Omega" (Rv 1:8; 21:6), "the beginning and the end" (Rv 21:6). In Him the Father has spoken the definitive word about mankind and its history. This is expressed in a concise and powerful way by the Letter to the Hebrews: "In many and various ways God spoke of old to our fathers by the prophets; *but in these last days he has spoken to us by a Son"* (1:1-2).

6. Jesus was born of the Chosen People, in fulfillment of the promise made to Abraham and constantly recalled by the Prophets. The latter spoke in God's name and in his place. The economy of the Old Testament, in fact, was essentially ordered to preparing and proclaiming the coming of Christ, the Redeemer of the universe, and of his Messianic Kingdom. The books of the Old Covenant are thus a permanent witness to a careful divine pedagogy.[8] *In Christ* this pedagogy achieves its purpose: Jesus does not in fact merely speak in the name of God like the Prophets, but he is God Himself speaking in His Eternal Word made flesh. Here we touch upon *the essential point by which Christianity differs from all the other religions,* by which *man's search for God* has been expressed from earliest times. Christianity has its starting point in the Incarnation of the Word. Here it is not simply a case of man seeking God, but of

God who comes in Person to speak to man of Himself and to show him the path by which He may be reached. This is what is proclaimed in the Prologue of John's Gospel: "No one has ever seen God; the only Son, who is in the bosom of the Father, he has made him known" (1:18). *The Incarnate Word is thus the fulfillment of the yearning present in all the religions of mankind:* This fulfillment is brought about by God Himself and transcends all human expectations. It is the mystery of grace.

In Christ, religion is no longer a "blind search for God" (cf. Acts 17:27) but the *response of faith* to God who reveals Himself. It is a response in which man speaks to God as his Creator and Father, a response made possible by that one Man who is also the consubstantial Word in whom God speaks to each individual person and by whom each individual person is enabled to respond to God. What is more, in this Man all creation responds to God. Jesus Christ is the new beginning of everything. In Him all things come into their own; they are taken up and given back to the Creator from whom they first came. *Christ is thus the fulfillment of the yearning of all the world's religions and, as such, He is their sole and definitive completion.* Just as God in Christ speaks to humanity of Himself, so in Christ all humanity and the whole of creation speaks of itself to God—indeed, it gives itself to God. Everything thus returns to its origin. *Jesus Christ is the recapitulation of everything* (cf. Eph 1:10) and at the same time the fulfillment of all things in God: a fulfillment which is the glory of God. The religion founded upon Jesus Christ is a *religion of glory;* it is a newness of life for the praise of the glory of God (cf.

Eph 1:12). All creation is in reality a manifestation of His glory. In particular, man (*vivens homo*) is the epiphany of God's glory, man who is called to live by the fullness of life in God.

7. *In Jesus Christ* God not only speaks to man but also *seeks him out.* The Incarnation of the Son of God attests that God goes in search of man. Jesus speaks of this search as the finding of a lost sheep (cf. Lk 15:1-7). It is a search which *begins in the heart of God* and culminates in the Incarnation of the Word. If God goes in search of man, created in His own image and likeness, He does so because He loves him eternally in the Word and wishes to raise him in Christ to the dignity of an adoptive son. God therefore goes in search of man who *is His special possession* in a way unlike any other creature. Man is God's possession by virtue of a choice made in love: God seeks man out, moved by His fatherly heart.

Why does God seek man out? Because man has turned away from Him, hiding himself as Adam did among the trees of the Garden of Eden (cf. Gn 3:8-10). *Man allowed himself to be led astray* by the enemy of God (cf. Gn 3:13). Satan deceived man, persuading him that he too was a god, that he, like God, was capable of knowing good and evil, ruling the world according to his own will without having to take into account the divine will (cf. Gn 3:5). Going in search of man through His Son, God wishes to persuade man to abandon the paths of evil which lead him farther and farther afield. "Making him abandon" those paths means making man understand that he is taking the wrong path; it means *overcoming the evil* which is everywhere found in human history. *Overcoming evil: this is the meaning of the Redemption.* This is brought about in the sacrifice of Christ, by which man redeems the debt of sin and is reconciled to God. The Son of God became man, taking a body and soul in the womb of the Virgin, precisely for this reason: to become the perfect redeeming sacrifice. The religion of the Incarnation is the *religion* of the world's Redemption through the sacrifice of Christ, wherein lies victory over evil, over sin, and over death itself. Accepting death on the Cross, Christ at the same time reveals and gives life because He rises again and death no longer has power over Him.

8. The religion which originates in the mystery of the Redemptive Incarnation is the religion of *"dwelling in the heart of God,"* of sharing in God's very life. St. Paul speaks of this in the passage already quoted: "God has sent the Spirit of his Son into our hearts, crying, 'Abba! Father!'" (Gal 4:6). Man cries out like Christ himself, who turned to God "with loud cries and tears" (Heb 5:7), especially in Gethsemane and on the Cross: man cries out to God just as Christ cried out to Him, and thus he bears witness that he shares in Christ's sonship through the power of the Holy Spirit. The Holy Spirit, whom the Father has sent in the name of the Son, enables man to share in the inmost life of God. He also enables man *to be a son, in the likeness of Christ,* and an heir of all that belongs to the Son (cf. Gal 4:7). In this consists the religion of "dwelling in the inmost life of God," which begins with the Incarnation of the Son of God. The Holy Spirit, who searches the depths of

God (cf. 1 Cor 2:10), leads us, all mankind, into these depths by virtue of the sacrifice of Christ.

II
THE JUBILEE OF THE YEAR 2000

9. Speaking of the birth of the Son of God, St. Paul places this event in the "fullness of time" (cf. Gal 4:4). *Time is indeed fulfilled by the very fact that God, in the Incarnation, came down into human history.* Eternity entered into time: what "fulfillment" could be greater than this? What other "fulfillment" would be possible? Some have thought in terms of certain *mysterious cosmic cycles* in which the history of the universe, and of mankind in particular, would constantly repeat itself. True, man rises from the earth and returns to it (cf. Gen 3:19): this is an immediately evident fact. Yet in man there is an irrepressible longing to live forever. How are we to imagine a life beyond death? Some have considered various forms of *reincarnation:* depending on one's previous life, one would receive a new life in either a higher or lower form until full purification is attained. This belief, deeply rooted in some Eastern religions, itself indicates that man rebels against the finality of death. He is convinced that his nature is essentially spiritual and immortal.

Christian Revelation excludes reincarnation, and speaks of a fulfillment which man is called to achieve in the course of a single earthly existence. Man achieves this fulfillment of his destiny through the sincere gift of self, a gift which is made possible only through his encounter with God. It is in God that man finds his full self-realization: *this is the truth revealed by Christ.* Man fulfills himself in God, who comes to meet him through his Eternal Son. Thanks to God's coming on earth, human time, which began at Creation, has reached its fullness. "The fullness of time" is in fact eternity, indeed, it is *the One who is eternal,* God Himself. Thus, to enter into "the fullness of time" means to reach the end of time and to transcend its limits, in order to find time's fulfillment in the eternity of God.

10. *In Christianity time has a fundamental importance.* Within the dimension of time the world was created; within it the history of salvation unfolds, finding its culmination in the "fullness of time" of the Incarnation and its goal in the glorious return of the Son of God at the end of time. *In Jesus Christ, the Word made flesh, time becomes a dimension of God,* who is Himself eternal. With the coming of Christ there begin "the last days" (cf. Heb 1:2), the "last hour" (cf. 1 Jn 2:18), and the time of the Church, which will last until the Parousia.

From this relationship of God with time there arises *the duty to sanctify time.* This is done, for example, when individual times, days, or weeks are dedicated to God, as once happened in the religion of the Old Covenant, and as happens still, though in a new way, in Christianity. In the liturgy of the Easter Vigil the celebrant, as he blesses the candle which symbolizes the risen Christ, proclaims: "Christ yesterday and today, the beginning and the end, Alpha and Omega, all time belongs to him, and all the ages, to him be glory and power through every age for ever."

He says these words as he inscribes on the candle the numerals of the current year. The meaning of this rite is clear: It emphasizes the fact that *Christ is the Lord of time;* He is its beginning and its end; every year, every day, and every moment are embraced by his Incarnation and Resurrection, and thus become part of the "fullness of time." For this reason, the Church too lives and celebrates the liturgy in the span of a year. *The solar year is thus permeated by the liturgical year,* which in a certain way reproduces the whole mystery of the Incarnation and Redemption, beginning from the first Sunday of Advent and ending on the Solemnity of Christ the King, Lord of the Universe and Lord of History. Every Sunday commemorates the day of the Lord's Resurrection.

11. Against this background we can understand *the Custom of Jubilees,* which began in the Old Testament and continues in the history of the Church. Jesus of Nazareth, going back one day to the *synagogue of his hometown,* stood up to read (cf. Lk 4:16-30). Taking the book of the Prophet Isaiah, he read this passage: "The Spirit of the Lord God is upon me, because the Lord has anointed me to bring good tidings to the afflicted; he has sent me to bind up the brokenhearted, to proclaim liberty to the captives, and the opening of the prison to those who are bound; *to proclaim the year of the Lord's favor"* (61:1-2).

The Prophet was speaking of the Messiah. "Today," Jesus added, "this scripture has been fulfilled in your hearing" (Lk 4:21), thus indicating that He Himself was the Messiah foretold by the prophet, and that the long-expected "time" was beginning in

Him. The day of salvation had come, the "fullness of time." *All Jubilees point to this "time" and refer to the Messianic mission of Christ,* who came as the one "anointed" by the Holy Spirit, the one "sent by the Father." It is He who proclaims the good news to the poor. It is He who brings liberty to those deprived of it, who frees the oppressed and gives back sight to the blind (cf. Mt 11:4-5; Lk 7:22). In this way He ushers in "a year of the Lord's favor," which He proclaims not only with His words but above all by His actions. The Jubilee, "a year of the Lord's favor," characterizes all the activity of Jesus; it is not merely the recurrence of an anniversary in time.

12. *The words and deeds of Jesus thus represent the fulfillment of the whole tradition of Jubilees* in the Old Testament. We know that the Jubilee was *a time dedicated in a special way to God.* It fell every seventh year, according to the Law of Moses: this was the "sabbatical year," during which the earth was left fallow and slaves were set free. The duty to free slaves was regulated by detailed prescriptions contained in the Books of Exodus (23:10-11), Leviticus (25:1-28), and Deuteronomy (15:1-6). In other words, these prescriptions are found in practically the whole of biblical legislation, which is thus marked by this very specific characteristic. In the sabbatical year, in addition to the freeing of slaves the Law also provided for the cancellation of all debts in accordance with precise regulations. And all this was to be done in honor of God. What was true for the sabbatical year was also true for the *Jubilee* year, which fell every fifty years. In the jubilee year, however, the customs of the sabbatical year were broadened and celebrated with even greater solemnity. As we read in Leviticus: "You shall hallow the 50th year and proclaim liberty throughout the land to all its inhabitants; it shall be a jubilee for you, when each of you shall return to his property and each of you shall return to his family" (25:10). One of the most significant consequences of the Jubilee year was the general *"emancipation" of all the dwellers on the land in need of being freed.* On this occasion every Israelite regained possession of his ancestral land, if he happened to have sold it or lost it by falling into slavery. He could never be completely deprived of the land, because it belonged to God; nor could the Israelites remain forever in a state of slavery, since God had "redeemed" them for Himself as His exclusive possession by freeing them from slavery in Egypt.

13. The prescriptions for the Jubilee year largely remained ideals—more a hope than an actual fact. They thus became a *prophetia futuri* insofar as they foretold the freedom which would be won by the coming Messiah. Even so, on the basis of the juridical norms contained in these prescriptions a kind of *social doctrine* began to emerge, which would then more clearly develop beginning with the New Testament. *The Jubilee year was meant to restore equality among all the children of Israel,* offering new possibilities to families which had lost their property and even their personal freedom. On the other hand, the Jubilee year was a reminder to the rich that a time would come when their Israelite slaves would once again become their equals and would be able to reclaim their rights. At the times prescribed by Law, a Jubilee year had to be proclaimed, to assist those in need. This was required by just government. *Justice, according to the Law of Israel, consisted above all in the protection of the weak,* and a king was supposed to be outstanding in this regard, as the psalmist says: "He delivers the needy when he calls, the poor and him who has no helper. He has pity on the weak and the needy, and saves the lives of the needy" (Ps 72:12-13). *The foundations of this tradition were strictly theological,* linked first of all with the theology of Creation and with that of Divine Providence. It was a common conviction, in fact, that *to God alone, as Creator, belonged the "dominium altum"*—lordship over all creation and over the earth in particular (cf. Lv 25:23). If in His Providence God had given the earth to humanity, that meant that He had given it to everyone. Therefore *the riches of Creation were to be considered as a common good of the whole of humanity.* Those who possessed these goods as personal property were really only stewards, ministers charged with working in the name of God, who remains the sole owner in the full sense, since it is God's will that created goods should serve everyone in a just way. *The Jubilee year was meant to restore this social justice.* The social doctrine of the Church, which has always been a part of Church teaching and which has developed greatly in the last century, particularly after the encyclical *Rerum Novarum,* is rooted in the tradition of the Jubilee year.

14. What needs to be emphasized, however, is what Isaiah expresses in the words "*to proclaim the year of the Lord's favor.*" For the Church, the Jubilee is precisely this "year of the Lord's favor," a year of the remission of sins and of the punishments due to them, a year of reconciliation between disputing parties, a year of manifold conversions and of sacramental and extra-sacramental penance. The tradition of Jubilee years involves the *granting* of indulgences on a larger scale than at other times. Together with Jubilees recalling the mystery of the Incarnation, at intervals of one hundred, fifty, and twenty-five years, there are also Jubilees which commemorate the event of the Redemption: the Cross of Christ, his death on Golgotha, and the Resurrection. On these occasions, the Church proclaims "a year of the Lord's favor," and she tries to ensure that all the faithful can benefit from this grace. *That is why Jubilees are celebrated not only "in Urbe" but also "extra Urbem":* traditionally the latter took place the year after the celebration "in Urbe."

15. *In the lives of individuals, Jubilees* are usually connected with the date of birth; but other anniversaries are also celebrated such as those of Baptism, Confirmation, First Communion, Priestly or Episcopal Ordination, and the Sacrament of Marriage. Some of these anniversaries have parallels in the secular world, but Christians always give them a religious character. In fact, in the Christian view every Jubilee—the 25th of Marriage or Priesthood, known as "silver," the 50th, known as "golden," or the 60th, known as "diamond"—is a *particular year of favor* for the individual who has received one or other of the Sacraments. What we have said about individuals with regard to Jubilees can also be applied to *communities* *or institutions.* Thus we celebrate the centenary or the millennium of the foundation of a town or city. In the Church, we celebrate the Jubilees of parishes and dioceses. All these personal and community Jubilees have an important and significant role in the lives of individuals and communities.

In view of this, *the two thousand years which have passed since the birth of Christ* (prescinding from the question of its precise chronology) *represent an extraordinarily great Jubilee,* not only for Christians but indirectly for the whole of humanity, given the prominent role played by Christianity during these two millennia. It is significant that the calculation of the passing years begins almost everywhere with the year of Christ's coming into the world, which is thus *the center* of the calendar most widely used today. Is this not another sign of the unparalleled effect of the birth of Jesus of Nazareth on the history of mankind?

16. *The term "Jubilee" speaks of joy;* not just an inner joy but a jubilation which is manifested outwardly, for the coming of God is also an outward, visible, audible, and tangible event, as St. John makes clear (cf. 1 Jn 1:1). It is thus appropriate that every sign of joy at this coming should have its own outward expression. This will demonstrate that *the Church rejoices in salvation.* She invites everyone to rejoice, and she tries to create conditions to ensure that the power of salvation may be shared by all. Hence the Year 2000 will be celebrated as the Great Jubilee.

With regard to its *content, this Great Jubilee* will be, in a certain sense, like any other. But at the same time it will be different, greater than any other. For the Church respects the measurements of time: hours, days, years, centuries. She thus goes forward with every individual, helping everyone to realize how *each of these measurements of time is imbued with the presence of God* and with His saving activity. In this spirit the Church rejoices, gives thanks, and asks forgiveness, presenting her petitions to the Lord of history and of human consciences.

Among the most fervent petitions which the Church makes to the Lord during this important time, as the eve of the new millennium approaches, is that unity among all Christians of the various confessions will increase until they reach full communion. I pray that the Jubilee will be a promising opportunity for fruitful cooperation in the many areas which unite us; these are unquestionably more numerous than those which divide us. It would thus be quite helpful if, with due respect for the programs of the individual churches and communities, ecumenical agreements could be reached with regard to the preparation and celebration of the Jubilee. In this way the Jubilee will bear witness even more forcefully before the world that the disciples of Christ are fully resolved to reach full unity as soon as possible in the certainty that "nothing is impossible with God."

III
PREPARATION FOR THE GREAT JUBILEE

17. *In the Church's history every Jubilee is prepared for by Divine Providence.* This is true also of the Great Jubilee of the Year 2000. With this conviction, we look today with a sense of gratitude and yet with a sense of responsibility at all that has happened in human history since the birth of Christ, particularly the events which have occurred between the years 1000 and 2000. But in a very particular way, we look with the eyes of faith to our own century, searching out whatever bears witness not only to man's history but also to God's intervention in human affairs.

18. From this point of view we can affirm that *the Second Vatican Council was a providential event whereby the Church began the more immediate preparation* for the Jubilee of the second millennium. It was a Council similar to earlier ones, yet very different; it was a Council *focused on the mystery of Christ and his Church, and at the same time open to the world.* This openness was an evangelical response to recent changes in the world, including the profoundly disturbing experiences of the twentieth century, a century scarred by the First and Second World Wars, by the experience of concentration camps, and by horrendous massacres. All these events demonstrate most vividly that the world needs purification; it needs to be converted.

The Second Vatican Council is often considered as the beginning of a new era in the life of the Church. This is true, but at the same time it is difficult to overlook the fact that *the Council drew much from the experiences and reflections of the immediate past,* especially from the intellectual legacy left by Pius XII. In the history of the Church, the "old" and the "new" are always closely interwoven. The "new" grows out of the "old," and the "old" finds a fuller expression in the "new." Thus it was for the Second Vatican Council and for the activity of the popes connected with the Council, starting with John XXIII, continuing with Paul VI and John Paul I, up to the present pope.

What these popes have accomplished during and since the Council, in their Magisterium no less than in their pastoral activity, has certainly made a significant contribution to the *preparation of that new springtime of Christian life* which will be revealed by the Great Jubilee, if Christians are docile to the action of the Holy Spirit.

19. The Council, while not imitating the sternness of John the Baptist, who called for repentance and conversion on the banks of the Jordan (cf. Lk 3:1-7), did show something of the Prophet of old, pointing out with fresh vigor to the men and women of today that Jesus Christ is the "Lamb of God who takes away the sin of the world" (Jn 1:29), the Redeemer of humanity, and the Lord of history. During the Council, precisely out of a desire to be fully faithful to her Master, the Church questioned herself about her own identity and discovered anew the depth of her mystery as the Body and the Bride of Christ. Humbly heeding the Word of God, she reaffirmed the universal call to holiness; she made provision for the reform of the liturgy, the "origin and summit" of her life; she gave impetus to the renewal of many aspects of her life at the universal level and in the local churches; she strove to promote the various Christian vocations, from those of the laity to those of religious, from the ministry of deacons to that of priests and bishops; and in a particular way she rediscovered episcopal collegiality, that privileged expression of the pastoral service carried out by the bishops in communion with the successor of Peter. On the basis of this profound renewal, the Council opened itself to Christians of other denominations, to the followers of other religions, and to all the people of our time. No council had ever spoken so clearly about Christian unity, about dialogue with non-Christian religions, about the specific meaning of the Old Covenant and of Israel, about the dignity of each person's conscience, about the principle of religious liberty, about the different cultural traditions within which the Church carries out her missionary mandate, and about the means of social communication.

20. The Council's enormously rich body of teaching and *the striking new tone* in the way it presented this content constitute as it were a proclamation of new times. The Council Fathers spoke in the language of the Gospel, the language of the Sermon on the Mount and the Beatitudes. In the Council's message God is presented *in his absolute lordship over all things,* but also as *the One who ensures the authentic autonomy of earthly realities.*

The best preparation for the new millennium, therefore, can only be expressed in a renewed commitment *to apply,* as faithfully as possible, *the teachings of Vatican II to the life of every individual and of the whole Church.* It was with the Second Vatican Council that, in the broadest sense of the term, the immediate preparations for the Great Jubilee of the Year 2000 were really begun. If we look for an analogy in the liturgy, it could be said that the yearly *Advent liturgy* is the season nearest to the spirit of the Council. For

Advent prepares us to meet the One who was, who is, and who is to come (cf. Rv 4:8).

21. Part of the preparation for the approach of the year 2000 is the *series of Synods* begun after the Second Vatican Council: general Synods together with continental, regional, national and diocesan Synods. The theme underlying them all is *evangelization,* or rather the new evangelization, the foundations of which were laid down in the Apostolic Exhortation *Evangelii Nuntiandi* of Pope Paul VI, issued in 1975 following the Third General Assembly of the Synod of Bishops. These Synods themselves are part of the new evangelization: they were born of the Second Vatican Council's vision of the Church. They open up broad areas for the participation of the laity, whose specific responsibilities in the Church they define. They are an expression of the strength which Christ has given to the entire People of God, making it a sharer in His own Messianic mission as Prophet, Priest, and King. Very eloquent in this regard are the statements of the Dogmatic Constitution *Lumen Gentium. The preparation for the Jubilee year 2000 is thus taking place throughout the whole Church, on the universal and local levels,* giving her a new awareness of the salvific mission she has received from Christ. This awareness is particularly evident in the Post-Synodal Exhortations devoted to the mission of the laity, the formation of priests, catechesis, the family, the value of penance and reconciliation in the life of the Church and of humanity in general, as well as in the forthcoming one to be devoted to the consecrated life.

22. Special tasks and responsibilities with regard to the Great Jubilee of the year 2000 belong to the *ministry of the Bishop of Rome*. In a certain sense, all the popes of the past century have prepared for this Jubilee. With his program to renew all things in Christ, St. Pius X tried to forestall the tragic developments which arose from the international situation at the beginning of this century. The Church was aware of her duty to act decisively to promote and defend the basic values of peace and justice in the face of contrary tendencies in our time. The Popes of the period before the Council acted with firm commitment, each in his own way: Benedict XV found himself faced with the tragedy of the First World War; Pius XI had to contend with the threats of totalitarian systems or systems which did not respect human freedom in Germany, in Russia, in Italy, in Spain, and even earlier still in Mexico. Pius XII took steps to counter the very grave injustice brought about by a total contempt for human dignity at the time of the Second World War. He also provided enlightened guidelines for the birth of a new world order after the fall of the previous political systems.

Furthermore, in the course of this century the Popes, following in the footsteps of Leo XIII, systematically developed the themes of Catholic social doctrine, expounding the characteristics of a *just system* in the area of relations between labor and capital. We may recall the encyclical *Quadragesimo Anno* of Pius XI, the numerous interventions of Pius XII, the encyclicals *Mater et Magistra* and *Pacem in Terris* of John XXIII, the Encyclical *Populorum Progressio* and the apostolic letter *Octogesima Adveniens* of Paul VI. I too have frequently dealt with this subject. I specifically devoted the encyclical *Laborem Exercens* to the importance of human labor, while in *Centesimus Annus* I wished to reaffirm the relevance, one hundred years later, of the doctrine presented in *Rerum Novarum*. In my encyclical *Sollicitudo Rei Socialis* I had earlier offered a systematic reformulation of the Church's entire social doctrine against the background of the East-West confrontation and the danger of nuclear war. The two elements of the Church's social doctrine—the *safeguarding of human dignity and rights* in the sphere of a just relation between labor and capital, and *the promotion of peace*—were closely joined in this text. The papal messages of 1 January each year, begun in 1968 in the pontificate of Paul VI, are also meant to serve the cause of peace.

23. Since the publication of the very first document of my Pontificate, *I have spoken explicitly of the Great Jubilee,* suggesting that the time leading up to it be lived as "a new Advent."[9] This theme has since reappeared many times, and was dwelt upon at length in the encyclical *Dominum et Vivificantem.*[10] In fact, preparing for the *year 2000 has become as it were a hermeneutical key of my Pontificate.* It is certainly not a matter of indulging in a new millenarianism, as occurred in some quarters at the end of the first millennium; rather, it is *aimed at an increased sensitivity to all that the Spirit is saying to the Church and to the churches* (cf. Rv 2:7 ff.), as well as to individuals through charisms meant to serve the whole community. The purpose is to emphasize what the Spirit is suggesting to the different communities, from the smallest ones, such as the family, to the largest ones, such as nations and international organizations, taking into account cultures, societies, and sound traditions. Despite appearances, humanity continues to await the revelation of the children of God and lives by this hope, like a mother in labor, to use the image employed so powerfully by St. Paul in his Letter to the Romans (cf. 8:19-22).

24. *Papal journeys* have become an important element in the work of implementing the Second Vatican Council. Begun by John XXIII on the eve of the Council with a memorable pilgrimage to Loreto and Assisi (1962), they notably increased under Paul VI, who after first visiting the Holy Land (1964) undertook nine other great apostolic journeys which brought him into direct contact with the peoples of the different continents.

The current Pontificate has widened this program of travels even further, starting with Mexico, on the occasion of the Third General Conference of the Latin American Episcopate held in Puebla in 1979. In that same year there was also the trip to Poland for the Jubilee of the nine hundredth anniversary of the death of St. Stanislaus, bishop and martyr.

The successive stages of these travels are well known. Papal journeys have become a regular occurrence, taking in the particular churches in every continent and showing concern *for the development of ecumenical relationships* with Christians of various denominations. Particularly important in this regard were the visits to Turkey (1979), Germany (1980), England, Scotland, and Wales (1982),

Switzerland (1984), the Scandinavian countries (1989), and most recently the Baltic countries (1993).

At present, it is my fervent wish to visit Sarajevo in Bosnia-Herzegovina and the Middle East: Lebanon, Jerusalem, and the Holy Land. It would be very significant if in the year 2000 it were possible to visit the *places on the road taken by the People of God of the Old Covenant,* starting from the places associated with Abraham and Moses, through Egypt and Mount Sinai, as far as Damascus, the city which witnessed the conversion of St. Paul.

25. In preparing for the year 2000, *the individual churches* have their own role to play, as they celebrate with their own Jubilees significant stages in the salvation history of the various peoples. Among these regional or *local Jubilees,* events of great importance have included the millennium of the Baptism of Rus' in 1988[11] as also the five hundredth anniversary of the beginning of evangelization in America (1492). Besides events of such wide-ranging impact, we may recall others which, although not of universal importance, are no less significant: for example, the millennium of the Baptism of Poland in 1966 and of the Baptism of Hungary in 1968, together with the six hundredth anniversary of the Baptism of Lithuania in 1987. There will soon also be celebrated the fifteen hundredth anniversary of the baptism of Clovis (496), King of the Franks, and the fourteen hundredth anniversary of the arrival of St. Augustine in Canterbury (597), marking the beginning of the evangelization of the Anglo-Saxon world.

As far as Asia is concerned, the Jubilee will remind

us of the Apostle Thomas, who, according to tradition, brought the proclamation of the Gospel at the very beginning of the Christian era to India, where missionaries from Portugal would not arrive until about the year 1500. The current year also marks the seventh centenary of the evangelization of China (1294), and we are preparing to commemorate the spread of missionary work in the Philippines with the erection of the Metropolitan See of Manila (1595). We likewise look forward to the fourth centenary of the first martyrs in Japan (1597).

In Africa, where the first proclamation of the Gospel also dates back to apostolic times, together with the 1,650th anniversary of the episcopal consecration of the first bishop of the Ethiopians, St. Frumentius (c. 340), and the five hundredth anniversary of the beginning of the evangelization of Angola in the ancient Kingdom of the Congo (1491), nations such as Cameroon, Côte d'Ivoire, the Central African Republic, Burundi and Burkina Faso are celebrating the centenaries of the arrival of the first missionaries in their respective territories. Other African nations have recently celebrated such centenaries.

And how can we fail to mention the Eastern Churches, whose ancient Patriarchates are so closely linked to the apostolic heritage and whose venerable theological, liturgical, and spiritual traditions constitute a tremendous wealth which is the common patrimony of the whole of Christianity? The many Jubilee celebrations in these churches and in the communities which acknowledge them as the origin of their own apostolicity recall the journey of Christ down the centuries, leading to the Great Jubilee at the end of the second millennium.

Seen in this light, the whole of Christian history appears to us as a single river, into which many tributaries pour their waters. The year 2000 invites us to gather with renewed fidelity and ever deeper communion *along the banks of this great river:* the river of Revelation, of Christianity, and of the Church, a river which flows through human history starting from the event which took place at Nazareth and then at Bethlehem two thousand years ago. This is truly the "river" which with its "streams," in the expression of the psalm, "make glad the city of God" (46:4).

26. The *Holy Years* celebrated in the latter part of this century have also prepared for the year 2000. *The Holy Year* proclaimed by Paul VI in *1975* is still fresh in our memory. The celebration of *1983* as *the Year of Redemption* followed along the same lines. *The Marian Year 1986/87* perhaps struck a more resounding chord; it was eagerly awaited and profoundly experienced in the individual local churches, especially at the Marian shrines around the world. The encyclical *Redemptoris Mater,* issued on that occasion, drew attention to the Council's teaching on the presence of the Mother of God in the mystery of Christ and the Church: two thousand years ago the Son of God was made man by the power of the Holy Spirit and was born of the Immaculate Virgin Mary. *The Marian Year was as it were an anticipation of the Jubilee,* and contained much of what will find fuller expression in the year 2000.

27. It would be difficult not to recall that the Marian Year took place only shortly before *the events of 1989.* Those events remain surprising for their vastness and especially for the speed with which they occurred. The '80s were years marked by a growing danger from the "Cold War." 1989 ushered in a peaceful resolution which took the form, as it were, of an "organic" development. In the light of this fact, we are led to recognize a truly prophetic significance in the encyclical *Rerum Novarum:* everything that Pope Leo XIII wrote there about Communism was borne out by these events, as I emphasized in the encyclical *Centesimus Annus.*[12] In the unfolding of those events one could already discern the invisible hand of Providence at work with maternal care: "Can a woman forget her infant?" (cf. Is 49:15).

After 1989 however there arose *new dangers and threats.* In the countries of the former Eastern bloc, after the fall of Communism, there appeared the serious threat of exaggerated nationalism, as is evident from events in the Balkans and other neighboring areas. This obliges the European nations to make a serious *examination of conscience* and to acknowledge faults and errors, both economic and political, resulting from imperialist policies carried out in the previous and present centuries vis-à-vis nations whose rights have been systematically violated.

28. In the wake of the Marian Year, we are now observing *the Year of the Family,* a celebration which is closely connected with the mystery of the Incarnation and with the very history of humanity. Thus there is good cause to hope that the Year of the

Family, inaugurated at Nazareth, will become, like the Marian Year, *another significant stage in preparation for the Great Jubilee.*

With this in view, I wrote a *Letter to Families,* the purpose of which was to restate the substance of the Church's teaching on the family and to bring this teaching, so to speak, into every home. At the Second Vatican Council, the Church recognized her duty to promote the dignity of marriage and the family.[13] The Year of the Family is meant to help make the Council's teaching in this regard a reality. *Each family, in some way, should be involved in the preparation for the Great Jubilee.* Was it not through a family, the family of Nazareth, that the Son of God chose to enter into human history?

IV
IMMEDIATE PREPARATION

29. Against the background of this sweeping panorama a question arises: Can we draw up *a specific program* of initiatives for the *immediate preparation* of the Great Jubilee? In fact, what has been said above already includes some elements of such a program.

A more detailed plan of specific events will call for widespread consultation in order for it not to be artificial and difficult to implement in the particular churches, which live in such different conditions. For this reason I wished to consult the Presidents of the Episcopal Conferences and especially the Cardinals.

I am grateful to the members of the College of Cardinals who met in Extraordinary Consistory on 13-14 June 1994, considered numerous proposals, and suggested helpful guidelines. I also thank my brothers in the Episcopate who in various ways communicated valuable ideas, which I have kept carefully in mind while writing this apostolic letter.

30. The first recommendation which clearly emerged from the consultation regards *the period of preparation.* Only a few years now separate us from the year 2000: it seemed fitting to divide this period into *two phases,* reserving the *strictly preparatory* phase for the last three years. It was thought that the accumulation of many activities over the course of a longer period of preparation would detract from its spiritual intensity.

It was therefore considered appropriate to approach the historic date with a *first phase,* which would make the faithful aware of general themes, and then to concentrate the direct and immediate preparation into a *second phase* consisting of a *three-year period* wholly directed to the celebration of the mystery of Christ the Savior.

A) First Phase

31. *The first phase* will therefore be of an *ante-preparatory* character; it is meant to revive in the Christian people an awareness of the value and meaning of the Jubilee of the year 2000 *in human history.* As a commemoration of the birth of Christ, the Jubilee is *deeply charged with Christological significance.*

In keeping with the unfolding of the Christian faith in word and sacrament, it seems important, even in this special anniversary, to link the structure of *memorial* with that of *celebration,* not limiting commemoration of the event only to ideas but also making its saving significance present through the celebration of the sacraments. The Jubilee celebration should confirm the Christians of today in their *faith* in God who has revealed himself in Christ, sustain their *hope* which reaches out in expectation of eternal life, and rekindle their *charity* in active service to their brothers and sisters.

During the first stage (1994 to 1996) the Holy See, through a special *Committee* established for this purpose, will suggest courses of reflection and action at the universal level. A similar commitment to promoting awareness will be carried out in a more detailed way by corresponding *commissions in the local churches*. In a way, it is a question of continuing what was done in the period of remote preparation and at the same time of *coming to a deeper appreciation of the most significant aspects of the Jubilee celebration*.

32. A Jubilee is always an occasion of special grace, "a day blessed by the Lord." As has already been noted, it is thus a time of joy. The Jubilee of the year 2000 is meant to be a great *prayer of praise and thanksgiving*, especially for the *gift of the Incarnation of the Son of God and of the Redemption* which He accomplished. In the Jubilee year Christians will stand with the renewed wonder of faith before the love of the Father, who *gave His Son*, "that whoever believes in him should not perish but have eternal life" (Jn 3:16). With a profound sense of commitment, they will likewise express their gratitude for the *gift of the Church*, established by Christ as "a kind of sacrament or sign of intimate union with God, and of the unity of all mankind."[14] Their thanksgiving will embrace the *fruits of holiness* which have matured in the life of all those many men and women who in every generation and every period of history have fully welcomed the gift of Redemption.

Nevertheless, the joy of every Jubilee is above all a *joy based upon the forgiveness of sins, the joy of conversion.* It therefore seems appropriate to emphasize once more the theme of the *Synod of Bishops in 1984: penance and reconciliation.*[15] That synod was an event of extraordinary significance in the life of the post-conciliar Church. It took up the ever topical question of conversion (*metanoia*), which is the precondition for reconciliation with God on the part of both individuals and communities.

33. Hence it is appropriate that, as the second millennium of Christianity draws to a close, the Church should become more fully conscious of the sinfulness of her children, recalling all those times in history when they departed from the spirit of Christ and his Gospel and, instead of offering to the world the witness of a life inspired by the values of faith, indulged in ways of thinking and acting which were truly *forms of counter-witness and scandal.*

Although she is holy because of her incorporation into Christ, the Church does not tire of doing penance: Before God and man *she always acknowledges as her own her sinful sons and daughters.* As *Lumen Gentium* affirms: "The Church, embracing sinners to her bosom, is at the same time holy and always in need of being purified, and incessantly pursues the path of penance and renewal."[16]

The Holy Door of the Jubilee of the year 2000 should be symbolically wider than those of previous Jubilees, because humanity, upon reaching this goal, will leave behind not just a century but a millennium. It is fitting that the Church should make this passage with a clear awareness of what has happened to her during the last ten centuries. She cannot cross the threshold of the new millennium without encouraging her children to purify themselves, through repentance, of past errors and instances of infidelity, inconsistency, and slowness to act. Acknowledging the weaknesses of the past is an act of honesty and courage which helps us to strengthen our faith, which alerts us to face today's temptations and challenges and prepares us to meet them.

34. Among the sins which require a greater commitment to repentance and conversion should certainly be counted those which *have been detrimental to the unity willed by God for His People.* In the course of the thousand years now drawing to a close, even more than in the first millennium, ecclesial communion has been painfully wounded, a fact "for which, at times, men of both sides were to blame."[17] Such wounds openly contradict the will of Christ and are a cause of scandal to the world.[18] These sins of the past unfortunately still burden us and remain ever present temptations. It is necessary to make amends for them, and earnestly to beseech Christ's forgiveness.

In these last years of the millennium, the Church should invoke the Holy Spirit with ever greater insistence, imploring from Him the grace of *Christian unity.* This is a crucial matter for our testimony to the

Gospel before the world. Especially since the Second Vatican Council many ecumenical initiatives have been undertaken with generosity and commitment: it can be said that the whole activity of the local churches and of the Apostolic See has taken on an ecumenical dimension in recent years. The *Pontifical Council for the Promotion of Christian Unity* has become an important catalyst in the movement toward full unity.

We are all however aware that the attainment of this goal cannot be the fruit of human efforts alone, vital though they are. *Unity, after all, is a gift of the Holy Spirit.* We are asked to respond to this gift responsibly, without compromise in our witness to the truth, generously implementing the guidelines laid down by the Council and in subsequent documents of the Holy See, which are also highly regarded by many Christians not in full communion with the Catholic Church.

This then is one of the tasks of Christians as we make our way to the year 2000. The approaching end of the second millennium demands of everyone an *examination of conscience* and the promotion of fitting ecumenical initiatives, so that we can celebrate the Great Jubilee, if not completely united, *at least much closer to overcoming the divisions of the second millen-nium.* As everyone recognizes, an enormous effort is needed in this regard. It is essential not only to continue along the path of dialogue on doctrinal matters, but above all to be more committed to *prayer for Christian unity.* Such prayer has become much more intense after the Council, but it must increase still more, involving an ever greater number of Christians, in unison with the great petition of Christ before his Passion: "Father... that they also may all be one in us" (cf. Jn 17:21).

35. Another painful chapter of history to which the sons and daughters of the Church must return with a spirit of repentance is that of the acquiescence given, especially in certain centuries, to *intolerance and even the use of violence* in the service of truth.

It is true that an accurate historical judgment cannot prescind from careful study of the cultural conditioning of the times, as a result of which many people may have held in good faith that an authentic witness to the truth could include suppressing the opinions of others or at least paying no attention to them. Many factors frequently converged to create assumptions which justified intolerance and fostered an emotional climate from which only great spirits, truly free and filled with God, were in some way able to break free. Yet the consideration of mitigating factors does not exonerate the Church from the obligation to express profound regret for the weaknesses of so many of her sons and daughters who sullied her face, preventing her from fully mirroring the image of her crucified Lord, the supreme witness of patient love and of humble meekness. From these painful moments of the past a lesson can be drawn for the future, leading all Christians to adhere fully to the sublime principle stated by the Council: "The truth cannot impose itself except by virtue of its own truth, as it wins over the mind with both gentleness and power."[19]

36. Many cardinals and bishops expressed the desire for a serious examination of conscience above all on the part of *the Church of today*. On the threshold of the new millennium Christians need to place themselves humbly before the Lord and examine themselves on *the responsibility which they too have for the evils of our day*. The present age in fact, together with much light, also presents not a few shadows.

How can we remain silent, for example, about the *religious indifference* which causes many people today to live as if God did not exist or to be content with a vague religiosity, incapable of coming to grips with the question of truth and the requirement of consistency? To this must also be added the widespread loss of the transcendent sense of human life and confusion in the ethical sphere, even about the fundamental values of respect for life and the family. The sons and daughters of the Church, too, need to examine themselves in this regard. To what extent have they been shaped by the climate of secularism and ethical relativism? And what responsibility do they bear, in view of the increasing lack of religion, for not having shown the true face of God, by having "failed in their religious, moral or social life"?[20]

It cannot be denied that for many Christians the spiritual life is passing through *a time of uncertainty* which affects not only their moral life but also their life of prayer and the *theological correctness of their faith*. Faith, already put to the test by the challenges of our times, is sometimes disoriented by erroneous theological views, the spread of which is abetted by the crisis of obedience vis-à-vis the Church's Magisterium.

And with respect to the Church of our time, how can we not lament *the lack of discernment,* which at times became even acquiescence, shown by many Christians concerning the violation of fundamental human rights by totalitarian regimes? And should we not also regret, among the shadows of our own day, the responsibility shared by so many Christians *for grave forms of injustice and exclusion?* It must be asked how many Christians really know and put into practice the principles of the Church's social doctrine.

An examination of conscience must also consider *the reception given to the Council,* this great gift of the Spirit to the Church at the end of the second millennium. To what extent has the Word of God become more fully the soul of theology and the inspiration of the whole of Christian living, as *Dei Verbum* sought? Is the liturgy lived as the "origin and summit" of ecclesial life, in accordance with the teaching of *Sacrosanctum Concilium?* In the universal Church and in the particular churches, is the ecclesiology of communion described in *Lumen Gentium* being strengthened? Does it leave room for charisms, ministries, and different forms of participation by the People of God, without adopting notions borrowed from democracy and sociology which do not reflect the Catholic vision of the Church and the authentic spirit of Vatican II? Another serious question is raised by the nature of relations between the Church and the world. The Council's guidelines—set forth in *Guadium et Spes* and other documents—of open, respectful, and cordial dialogue, yet accompanied by careful discernment and courageous witness to the truth, remain valid and call us to a greater commitment.

37. The Church of the first millennium was born of the blood of the martyrs: *"Sanguis martyrum—semen christianorum."*[21] The historical events linked to the figure of Constantine the Great could never have ensured the development of the Church as it occurred during the first millennium if it had not been for the *seeds sown by the martyrs and the heritage of sanctity which marked the first Christian generations.* At the end of the second millennium, *the Church has once again become a Church of martyrs.* The persecutions of believers—priests, religious, and laity—has caused a great sowing of martyrdom in different parts of the world. The witness to Christ borne even to the shedding of blood has become a common inheritance of Catholics, Orthodox, Anglicans, and Protestants, as Pope Paul VI pointed out in his homily for the canonization of the Ugandan martyrs.[22]

This witness must not be forgotten. The Church of the first centuries, although facing considerable organizational difficulties, took care to write down in special martyrologies. Theses martyrologies have been constantly updated through the centuries, and the register of the saints and the blessed bears the names not only of those who have shed their blood for Christ but also of teachers of the faith, missionaries, confessors, bishops, priests, virgins, married couples, widows, and children.

In our own century the martyrs have returned, many of them nameless, *"unknown soldiers"* as it were *of God's great cause.* As far as possible, their witness should not be lost to the Church. As was recommended in the Consistory, *the local churches should do everything possible to ensure that the memory of those who have suffered martyrdom should be safeguarded, gathering the necessary documentation.* This gesture cannot fail to have an ecumenical character and expression. Perhaps the most convincing form of ecumenism is *the ecumenism of the saints* and of the martyrs. The *communio sanctorum* speaks louder than the things which divide us. The *martyrologium* of the first centuries was the basis of the veneration of the saints. By proclaiming and venerating the holiness of her sons and daughters, the Church gave supreme honor to God Himself; in the martyrs she venerated Christ, who was at the origin of their martyrdom and of their holiness. In later times there developed the practice of canonization, a practice which still continues in the Catholic Church and in the Orthodox Churches. In recent years the number of canonizations and beatifications has increased. These show *the vitality of the local churches,* which are much more numerous today than in the first centuries and in the first millennium. The greatest homage which all the churches can give to Christ on the threshold of the third millennium will be to manifest the Redeemer's all-powerful presence through the fruits of faith, hope, and charity present in men and women of many different tongues and races who have followed Christ in the various forms of the Christian vocation.

It will be the task of the Apostolic See, in preparation for the year 2000, *to update the martyrologies* for the universal Church, paying careful attention to the holiness of those who *in our own time* lived fully by the truth of Christ. In particular, there is a need to foster the recognition of the heroic virtues of men and women who have lived their Christian vocation *in marriage.* Precisely because we are convinced of the abundant fruits of holiness in the married state, we need to find the most appropriate means for discerning them and proposing them to the whole Church as a model and encouragement for other Christian spouses.

38. A further need emphasized by the cardinals and bishops is that of *continental synods,* following the example of those already held for Europe and Africa. The last General Conference of the Latin American Episcopate accepted, in agreement with the bishops of North America, the proposal for *a Synod for the Americas* on the problems of the new evangelization in both parts of the same continent, so different in origin and history, and on issues of justice and of international economic relations, in view of the enormous gap between North and South.

Another plan for a continent-wide synod will concern Asia, where the issue of the encounter of Christianity with ancient local cultures and religions is a pressing one. This is a great challenge for evangelization, since religious systems such as Buddhism or Hinduism have a clearly soteriological character. There is also an urgent need for a synod on the occasion of the Great Jubilee in order to illustrate and explain more fully the truth that Christ is the one Mediator between God and man and the sole Redeemer of the world, to be clearly distinguished from the founders of other great religions. With sincere esteem, the Church regards the elements of truth found in those religions as a reflection of the Truth which enlightens all men and women.[23] *"Ecce natus est nobis Salvator mundi*": In the year 2000 the proclamation of this truth should resound with renewed power.

Also for *Oceania* a regional synod could be useful. In this region there arises the question, among others, of the Aboriginal People, who in a unique way evoke aspects of human prehistory. In this synod a matter not to be overlooked, together with other problems of the region, would be the encounter of Christianity with the most ancient forms of religion, profoundly marked by a monotheistic orientation.

B) Second Phase

39. On the basis of this vast program aimed at creating awareness, it will then be possible to begin the *second phase,* the strictly *preparatory* phase. This will take place *over the span of three years,* from 1997 to 1999. The thematic structure of this three-year period, *centered on Christ,* the Son of God made man, must necessarily be theological, and therefore *Trinitarian.*

Year One: Jesus Christ

40. *The first year,* 1997, will thus be devoted to *reflection on Christ,* the Word of God, made man by the power of the Holy Spirit. *The distinctly Christological character of the Jubilee* needs to be emphasized, for it will celebrate the Incarnation and coming into the world of the Son of God, the mystery of salvation for all mankind. The general theme proposed by many cardinals and bishops for this year is: "Jesus Christ, the one Savior of the world, yesterday, today, and for ever" (cf. Heb 13:8).

Among the Christological themes suggested in the Consistory the following stand out: a renewed appreciation of Christ, Savior and Proclaimer of the Gospel, with special reference to the fourth chapter of the Gospel of Luke, where the theme of Christ's mission of preaching the Good News and the theme of the Jubilee are interwoven; a deeper understanding of the mystery of the Incarnation and of Jesus' birth from the Virgin Mary; the necessity of faith in Christ for salvation. In order to recognize who Christ truly is, Christians, especially in the course of this year, *should turn with renewed interest to the Bible,* "whether it be through the liturgy, rich in the divine Word, or through devotional reading, or through instructions suitable for the purpose and other aids."[24] In the revealed text it is the Heavenly Father Himself who comes to us in love and who dwells with us, disclosing to us the nature of His only-begotten Son and His plan of salvation for humanity.[25]

41. The commitment, mentioned earlier, to make the mystery of salvation sacramentally present can lead, in the course of the year, to a *renewed appreciation of Baptism* as the basis of Christian living, according to the words of the Apostle: "As many of you as were baptized into Christ have put on Christ" (Gal 3:27). The *Catechism of the Catholic Church,* for its part, recalls that Baptism constitutes "the foundation of communion among all Christians, including those who are not yet in full communion with the Catholic Church."[26] From an *ecumenical point of view,* this will certainly be a very important year for Christians to look together to Christ the one Lord, deepening our commitment to become one in Him, in accordance with His prayer to the Father. This emphasis on the centrality of Christ, of the Word of God, and of faith ought to inspire interest among Christians of other denominations and meet with a favorable response from them.

42. Everything ought to focus on the primary objective of the Jubilee: the *strengthening of faith and of the witness of Christians*. It is therefore necessary to inspire in all the faithful *a true longing for holiness,* a deep desire for conversion and personal renewal in a context of ever more intense prayer and of solidarity with one's neighbor, especially the most needy.

The first year therefore will be the opportune moment for a renewed appreciation of *catechesis* in its original meaning as "the Apostles' teaching" (Acts 2:42) about the Person of Jesus Christ and His mystery of salvation. In this regard, a detailed study of the *Catechism of the Catholic Church* will prove of great benefit, for the catechism presents "faithfully and systematically... the teaching of Sacred Scripture, the living Tradition of the Church and the authentic Magisterium, as well as the spiritual heritage of the Fathers, doctors and saints of the Church, to allow for a better knowledge of the Christian mystery and for enlivening the faith of the People of God."[27] To be realistic, we need to enlighten the consciences of the faithful concerning errors regarding the Person of Christ, clarifying objections against Him and against the Church.

43. *The Blessed Virgin,* who will be as it were "indirectly" present in the whole preparatory phase, will be contemplated in this first year especially in the mystery of her divine motherhood. It was in her womb that the Word became flesh! The affirmation of the central place of Christ cannot therefore be separated from the recognition of the role played by his Most Holy Mother. Veneration of her, when properly understood, can in no way take away from "the dignity and efficacy of Christ the one Mediator."[28] Mary in fact constantly points to her Divine Son and she is proposed to all believers as the *model of faith* which is put into practice. "Devotedly meditating on her and contemplating her in the light of the Word made man, the Church with reverence enters more intimately into the supreme mystery of the Incarnation and becomes ever increasingly like her Spouse."[29]

YEAR TWO: THE HOLY SPIRIT

44. 1998, the *second year* of the preparatory phase, will be dedicated in a particular way to the *Holy Spirit* and to His sanctifying presence within the community of Christ's disciples. "The *great Jubilee* at the close of the second millennium...," I wrote in the encyclical *Dominum et Vivificantem,* "has a *pneumatological aspect* since the mystery of the Incarnation was accomplished 'by the power of the Holy Spirit.' It was 'brought about' by that Spirit—consubstantial with the Father and the Son—who, in the absolute mystery of the Triune God, is the Person-love, the uncreated gift, who is the eternal source of every gift that comes from God in the order of creation, the direct principle and, in a certain sense, the subject of God's self-communication in the order of grace. The *mystery of the Incarnation constitutes the climax* of this giving, this divine self-communication."[30]

The Church cannot prepare for the new millennium "in any other way than *in the Holy Spirit.* What was accomplished by the power of the Holy Spirit 'in the fullness of time' can only through the Spirit's power now emerge from the memory of the Church."[31]

The Spirit, in fact, makes present in the Church of every time and place the unique Revelation brought by Christ to humanity, making it alive and active in the soul of each individual: "The Counselor, the Holy Spirit, whom the Father will send in my name, he will teach you all things, and bring to your remembrance all that I have said to you" (Jn 14:26).

45. The primary tasks of the preparation for the Jubilee thus include *a renewed appreciation of the presence and activity of the Spirit,* who acts within the Church both in the sacraments, especially in *Confirmation,* and in the variety of charisms, roles, and ministries which He inspires for the good of the Church: "There is only one Spirit who, according to his own richness and the needs of the ministries, distributes his different gifts for the welfare of the Church (cf. 1 Cor 12:1-11). Among these gifts stands out the grace given to the Apostles. To their authority, the Spirit Himself subjected even those who were endowed with charisms (cf. 1 Cor 14). Giving the body unity through Himself and through His power and through the internal cohesion of its members, this same Spirit produces and urges love among the believers."[32]

In our own day too, the Spirit is *the principal agent of the new evangelization*. Hence it will be important to gain a renewed appreciation of the Spirit as the One who builds the Kingdom of God within the course of history and prepares its full manifestation in Jesus Christ, stirring people's hearts and quickening in our world the seeds of the full salvation which will come at the end of time.

46. In this *eschatological perspective*, believers should be called to a renewed appreciation of the theological virtue *of hope*, which they have already heard proclaimed "in the word of the truth, the Gospel" (Col 1:5). The basic attitude of hope, on the one hand, encourages the Christian not to lose sight of the final goal which gives meaning and value to life, and on the other, offers solid and profound reasons for a daily commitment to transform reality in order to make it correspond to God's plan.

As the Apostle Paul reminds us: "We know that the whole creation has been groaning in travail together until now; and not only the creation, but we ourselves, who have the first fruits of the Spirit, groan inwardly as we wait for adoption as sons, the redemption of our bodies. For in this hope we were saved" (Rom 8:22-24). Christians are called to prepare for the Great Jubilee of the beginning of the third millennium *by renewing their hope in the definitive coming of the Kingdom of God,* preparing for it daily in their hearts, in the Christian community to which they belong, in their particular social context, and in world history itself.

There is also need for a better appreciation and understanding of *the signs of hope present in the last part of this century,* even though they often remain hidden from our eyes. *In society in general,* such signs of hope include: scientific, technological, and especially medical progress in the service of human life, a greater awareness of our responsibility for the environment, efforts to restore peace and justice wherever they have been violated, a desire for reconciliation and solidarity among different peoples, particularly in the complex relationship between the North and the South of the world. *In the Church,* they include a greater attention to the voice of the Spirit through the acceptance of charisms and the promotion of the laity, a deeper commitment to the cause of Christian unity, and the increased interest in dialogue with other religions and with contemporary culture.

47. The reflection of the faithful in the second year of preparation ought to focus particularly *on the value of unity* within the Church, to which the various gifts and charisms bestowed upon her by the Spirit are directed. In this regard, it will be opportune to promote a deeper understanding of the ecclesiological doctrine of the Second Vatican Council as contained primarily in the Dogmatic Constitution *Lumen Gentium.* This important document has expressly emphasized that the unity of the Body of Christ *is founded on the activity of the Spirit,* guaranteed by the apostolic ministry and sustained by mutual love (cf. 1 Cor 13:1-8). This catechetical enrichment of the faith cannot fail to bring the members of the People of God to a more mature awareness of their own responsibilities, as well as to a more lively sense of the importance of ecclesial obedience.[33]

48. *Mary,* who conceived the Incarnate Word by the power of the Holy Spirit and then in the whole of her life allowed herself to be guided by His interior activity, will be contemplated and imitated during this year above all as the woman who was docile to the voice of the Spirit, a woman of silence and attentiveness, a woman of hope who, like Abraham, accepted God's will "hoping against hope" (cf. Rom 4:18). Mary gave full expression to the longing of the poor of Yahweh and is a radiant model for those who entrust themselves with all their hearts to the promises of God.

YEAR THREE: GOD THE FATHER

49. 1999, *the third and final year of preparation,* will be aimed at broadening the horizons of believers so that they will see things in the perspective of Christ: *in the perspective of the "Father who is in heaven"* (cf. Mt 5:45), from whom the Lord was sent and to whom He has returned (cf. Jn 16:28).

"This is eternal life, that they know you the only true God, and Jesus Christ whom you have sent" (cf. Jn 17:3). The whole of the Christian life is like a great *pilgrimage to the house of the Father,* whose unconditional love for every human creature, and in particular for the "prodigal son" (cf. Lk 15:11-32), we discover anew each day. This pilgrimage takes place in the heart of each person, extends to the believing community, and then reaches to the whole of humanity.

The Jubilee, centered on the person of Christ, thus becomes a great act of praise to the Father: "Blessed be the God and Father of our Lord Jesus Christ, who has blessed us in Christ with every spiritual blessing in the heavenly places, even as he chose us in him before the foundation of the world, that we should be holy and blameless before him" (Eph 1:3-4).

50. In this third year the sense of being on a journey to the Father should encourage everyone to undertake, by holding fast to Christ the Redeemer of man, a journey of authentic *conversion*. This includes both a "negative" aspect, that of liberation from sin, and a "positive" aspect, that of choosing good, accepting the ethical values expressed in the natural law, which is confirmed and deepened by the Gospel. This is the proper context for a renewed appreciation and more intense celebration of the *Sacrament of Penance* in its most profound meaning. The call to conversion as the indispensable condition of Christian love is particularly important in contemporary society, where the very foundations of an ethically correct vision of human existence often seem to have been lost.

It will therefore be necessary, especially during this year, to emphasize the theological virtue of *charity*, recalling the significant and lapidary words of the First Letter of John: "God is love" (4:8, 16). Charity, in its twofold reality as love of God and neighbor, is the summing up of the moral life of the believer. It has in God its source and its goal.

51. From this point of view, if we recall that Jesus came to "preach the good news to the poor" (cf. Mt 11:5; Lk 7:22), how can we fail to lay greater emphasis on the *Church's preferential option for the poor and the outcast*? Indeed,it has to be said that a commitment to justice and peace in a world like ours, marked by so many conflicts and intolerable social and economic inequalities, is a necessary condition for the preparation and celebration of the Jubilee. Thus, in the spirit of the Book of Leviticus (25:8-12), Christians will have to raise their voice on behalf of all the poor of the world, proposing the Jubilee as an appropriate time to give thought, among other things, to reducing substantially, if not canceling outright, the international debt which seriously threatens the future of many nations. The Jubilee can also offer an opportunity for reflecting on other challenges of our time, such as the difficulties of dialogue between different cultures and the problems connected with respect for women's rights and the promotion of the family and marriage.

52. Recalling that "Christus,... by the revelation of the mystery of the Father and his love, fully reveals man to man himself and makes his supreme calling clear,"[34] two commitments should characterize in a special way the third preparatory year: *meeting the challenge of secularism and dialogue with the great religions.*

With regard to the former, it will be fitting to broach the vast subject of the *crisis of civilization,* which has become apparent especially in the West, which is highly developed from the standpoint of technology but is interiorly impoverished by its tendency to forget God or to keep Him at a distance. This crisis of civilization must be countered by *the civilization of love,* founded on the universal values of peace, solidarity, justice, and liberty, which find their full attainment in Christ.

53. On the other hand, as far as the field of religious awareness is concerned, the eve of the year 2000 will provide a great opportunity, especially in view of the events of recent decades, for *interreligious dialogue,* in accordance with the specific guidelines set down by the Second Vatican Council in its declaration *Nostra Aetate* on the relationship of the Church to non-Christian religions.

In this dialogue the Jews and the Muslims ought to have a preeminent place. God grant that as a confirmation of these intentions it may also be possible to hold *joint meetings* in places of significance for the great monotheistic religions.

In this regard, attention is being given to finding ways of arranging historic meetings in places of exceptional symbolic importance like Bethlehem, Jerusalem, and Mount Sinai as a means of furthering dialogue with Jews and the followers of Islam, and to arranging similar meetings elsewhere with the leaders of the great world religions. However, care will always have [to] be taken not to cause harmful misunderstandings, avoiding the risk of syncretism and of a facile and deceptive irenicism.

54. In this broad perspective of commitments, *Mary Most Holy,* the highly favored daughter of the Father, will appear before the eyes of believers as the perfect model of love toward both God and neighbor. As she herself says in the canticle of the *Magnificat*, great things were done for her by the Almighty, whose name is holy (cf. Lk 1:49). The Father chose her for a *unique mission* in the history of salvation: that of being the Mother of the long-awaited Savior. The Virgin Mary responded to God's call with complete openness: "Behold, I am the handmaid of the Lord" (Lk 1:38). Her motherhood, which began in Nazareth and was lived most intensely in Jerusalem at the foot of the Cross, will be felt during this year as a loving and urgent invitation addressed to all the children of God so that they will return to the house of the Father when they hear her maternal voice: "Do whatever Christ tells you" (cf. Jn 2:5).

C) Approaching the Celebration

55. A separate chapter will be the *actual celebration of the Great Jubilee,* which will take place simultaneously in the Holy Land, in Rome, and in the local churches throughout the world. Especially in this phase, the *phase of celebration,* the aim will be *to give glory to the Trinity,* from whom everything in the world and in history comes and to whom everything returns. This mystery is the focus of the three years of immediate preparation: from Christ and through Christ, in the Holy Spirit, to the Father. In this sense the Jubilee celebration makes present in an anticipatory way the goal and fulfillment of the life of each Christian and of the whole Church in the Triune God.

But since Christ is the only way to the Father, in order to highlight His living and saving presence in the Church and the world, the *International Eucharistic Congress* will take place in Rome, on the occasion of the Great Jubilee. The year 2000 will be intensely eucharistic: in the *Sacrament of the Eucharist* the Savior, who took flesh in Mary's womb twenty centuries ago, continues to offer Himself to humanity as the source of divine life.

The ecumenical and universal character of the sacred Jubilee can be fittingly reflected by a *meeting of all Christians*. This would be an event of great significance, and so, in order to avoid misunderstandings, it should be properly presented and carefully prepared, in an attitude of fraternal cooperation with Christians of other denominations and traditions, as well as of grateful openness to those religions whose representatives might wish to acknowledge the joy shared by all the disciples of Christ.

One thing is certain: Everyone is asked to do as much as possible to ensure that the great challenge of the year 2000 is not overlooked, for this challenge certainly involves a special grace of the Lord for the Church and for the whole of humanity.

V
CONCLUSION

56. The Church has endured for two thousand years. Like the *mustard seed* in the Gospel, she has grown and become a great tree, able to cover the whole of humanity with her branches (cf. Mt 13:31-32). The Second Vatican Council, in its Dogmatic Constitution on the Church, thus addresses the question of *membership in the Church and the call of all people* *to belong to the People of God:* "All are called to be part of this Catholic unity of the new People of God.... And there belong to it or are related to it in various ways the Catholic faithful as well as all who believe in Christ, and indeed the whole of mankind, which by the grace of God is called to salvation."[35] Pope Paul VI, in the encyclical *Ecclesiam Suam,* illustrates how all mankind is involved in the plan of God and emphasizes the various circles of the dialogue of salvation.[36]

Continuing this approach, we can also appreciate more clearly the Gospel parable of the leaven (cf. Mt 13:33): Christ, like a divine leaven, always and ever more fully penetrates the life of humanity, spreading the work of salvation accomplished in the Paschal Mystery. What is more, He embraces within His redemptive power *the whole past history* of the human race, beginning with the first Adam.[37] The *future* also belongs to Him: "Jesus Christ is the same yesterday and today and for ever" (Heb 13:8). For her part the Church "seeks but a solitary goal: to carry forward the work of Christ himself under the lead of the Holy Spirit, the Paraclete. And Christ entered this world to give witness to the truth, to rescue and not to sit in judgment, to serve and not to be served."[38]

57. Therefore, ever since the apostolic age *the Church's mission* has continued without interruption within the whole human family. The first evangelization took place above all in the region of the Mediterranean. In the course of the first millennium, missions setting out from Rome and Constantinople brought Christianity to *the whole conti-nent of Europe.* At the same time they made their way to the heart of *Asia,* as far as India and China. The end of the fifteenth century marked both the discovery of *America* and the beginning of the evangelization of those great continents, North and South. Simultaneously, while the sub-Saharan coasts of Africa welcomed the light of Christ, St. Francis Xavier, Patron of the Missions, reached Japan. At the end of the eighteenth century and the beginning of the nineteenth, a layman, Andrew Kim, brought Christianity to Korea. In the same period the proclamation of the Gospel reached Indochina, as well as *Australia and the islands of the Pacific.*

The nineteenth century witnessed vast missionary activity among the *peoples of Africa.* All these efforts bore fruit which has lasted up to the present day. The Second Vatican Council gives an account of this in the decree *Ad Gentes* on Missionary Activity. After the Council the question of missionary work was dealt with in the encyclical *Redemptoris Missio,* in the light of the problems of the missions in these final years of our century. In the future, too, the Church must continue to be missionary: Indeed missionary outreach is part of her very nature. With the fall of the great anti-Christian systems in Europe, first of Nazism and then of Communism, there is urgent need to bring once more the liberating message of the Gospel to the men and women of Europe.[39] Furthermore, as the encyclical *Redemptoris Missio* affirms, the modern world reflects the situation of the *Areopagus of Athens,* where St. Paul spoke.[40] Today there are many *"areopagi,"* and very different ones: These are the vast sectors of contemporary civilization and culture, of politics and economics. *The more the West is becoming estranged from its Christian roots, the more it is becoming missionary territory,* taking the form of many different *"areopagi."*

58. The future of the world and the Church belongs to the *younger generation,* to those who born in this century will reach maturity in the next, the first century of the new millennium. *Christ expects great things from young people,* as He did from the young man who asked Him: "What good deed must I do, to have eternal life?" (Mt 19:16). I have referred to the remarkable answer which Jesus gave to him in the recent encyclical *Veritatis Splendor,* as I did earlier, in 1985, in my *Apostolic Letter to the Youth of the World.* Young people, in every situation, in every region of the world, do not cease to put questions to Christ: *They meet Him and they keep searching for Him in order to question Him further.* If they succeed in following the road which He points out to them, they will have the joy of making their own contribution to His presence in the next century and in the centuries to come, until the end of time: "Jesus is the same yesterday, today, and for ever."

59. In conclusion, it is helpful to recall the words of the Pastoral Constitution *Gaudium et Spes:* "The Church believes that Christ, who died and was raised up for all, can through his Spirit offer man the light and the strength to measure up to his supreme destiny. Nor has any other name under heaven been given to man by which it is fitting for him to be saved. She likewise holds that *in her most benign Lord and Master can be found the key, the focal point and the* *goal of all human history.* The Church also maintains that beneath all changes there are *so many realities which do not change and which have their ultimate founda-tion in Christ,* who is the same yesterday and today and forever. Hence in the light of Christ, the image of the unseen God, the firstborn of every creature, the Council wishes to speak to all men in order to illuminate the mystery of man and to cooperate in finding the solution to the outstanding problems of our time."[41]

While I invite the faithful to raise to the Lord fervent prayers to obtain the light and assistance necessary for the preparation and celebration of the forthcoming Jubilee, I exhort my venerable brothers in the Episcopate and the ecclesial communities entrusted to them to open their hearts to the promptings of the Spirit. He will not fail to arouse enthusiasm and lead people to celebrate the Jubilee with renewed faith and generous participation.

I entrust this responsibility of the whole Church to the maternal intercession of Mary, Mother of the Redeemer. She, the Mother of Fairest Love, will be for Christians on the way to the Great Jubilee of the third millennium the star which safely guides their steps to the Lord. May the unassuming young woman of Nazareth, who two thousand years ago offered to the world the Incarnate Word, lead the men and women of the new millennium toward the One who is "the true light that enlightens every man" (Jn 1:9).

With these sentiments I impart to all my Blessing.

From the Vatican, on 10 November in the year 1994, the seventeenth of my pontificate.

NOTES

1997
YEAR ONE OF PREPARATION
Encountering God the Son

1. Vatican II, Dogmatic Constitution on the Church *Lumen Gentium*, 62.
2. *Lumen Gentium*, 6.
3. Ecumenical Council of Florence, *Decr. pro Armeniius, DS* 1314.
4. *Lumen Gentium*, 10.
5. *Lumen Gentium*, 9.
6. Vatican II, Decree on the Apostolate of Lay People *Apostolicam Actuositatem*, 4.
7. Vatican II, Dogmatic Constitution on Divine Revelation *Dei Verbum*, 25.
8. *Ennarat. in Ps.* CXXV, 5.
9. See *Summa Theologiae*, I-II, q. 69, a. 2; II-II, q. 8, a. 7.
10. *Decree on Ecumenism*, 7.

1998
YEAR TWO OF PREPARATION
Focusing on God the Holy Spirit

1. *Roman Missal*, Sequence for Easter Sunday.
2. *Lumen Gentium*, 68.
3. See St. Augustine, *De Civitate Dei*, XXII, 17: CCL48, 835f; St. Thomas Aquinas, *Summa Theologiae*, III pars., q. 64, art. 2 *ad tertium*.
4. *Lumen Gentium*, 39.
5. *Lumen Gentium*, 4.

6. John Paul II, The Apostolic Exhortation on the Family *Familiaris Consortio*, 33.
7. *Lumen Gentium*, 5.
8. *Lumen Gentium*, 5.
9. *Lumen Gaudium*, 28.
10. John Paul II, Apostolic Exhortation *Catechesi Tradendae*, 67: *AAS* 71 (1979), 1333.
11. Code of Canon Law, Can. 515,S 1.
12. *Lumen Gentium*, 15.
13. John Paul II, Homily at the Solemn Eucharistic Concelebration for the Close of the Seventh Ordinary General Assembly of the Synod of Bishops (October 30, 1987): *AAS* 80 (1988), 600.
14. *Lumen Gentium*, 37.
15. *Lumen Gentium*, 35.
16. *Lumen Gentium*, 12.
17. *Lumen Gentium*, 35.

1999
YEAR THREE OF PREPARATION
Returning to God the Father

1. St. Augustine, *In Iohannis Evangelium Tractatus*, 82, 3.
2. St. Augustine, *De Civitate Dei*, XIV, 28: *CCL* 48, p. 541.
3. John Paul II, Apostolic Exhortation *Reconciliatio et Paenitentia*, 18.
4. Vatican II, Pastoral Constitution on the Church in the Modern World *Gaudium et Spes*, 16.
5. *Gaudium et Spes*, 19.
6. *Lumen Gentium*, 11: *AAS* 57 (1965), 16.
7. Paul VI, Discourse to the Committee for the International Year of the Woman (April 18, 1975): *AAS* 67 (1975), 266.
8. John Paul II, Encyclical Letter *Sollicitudo Rei Socialis*, 34: *AAS* 80 (1988), 560.
9. *Gaudium et Spes*, 51.
10. Paul VI, *Address* at the Opening of the Second Session of the Second Vatican Ecumenical Council, September 29, 1963: *AAS* 55 (1963), 858.

11. Letter to the Fifth Plenary Assembly of Asian Bishops' Conferences (June 23, 1990), 4; *L'Osservatore Romano,* July 18, 1990.
12. Vatican II, Decree on the Missionary Activity of the Church *Ad Gentes,* 11, 15.
13. Vatican II, Declaration on the Church's Relations to Non-Christian Religions *Nostra Aetate,* 2.

As the Third Millennium Draws Near

1. Cf. Saint Bernard, *In Laudibus Virginis Matris, Homilia IV,* 8, *Opera Omnia,* Edit. Cister. (1966), 53.
2. *Gaudium et Spes,* 22.
3. *Gaudium et Spes,* 22.
4. Cf. *Ant. Iud.* 20:200, and the well-known and much-discussed passage in 18:63-64.
5. *Annales* 15:44, 3.
6. *Vita Claudii,* 25:4.
7. *Epist.* 10:96.
8. *Dei Verbum,* 15.
9. Encyclical Letter *Redemptor Hominis* (4 March 1979), 1: *AAS* 71 (1979), 258.
10. Cf. Encyclical Letter *Dominum et Vivificantem* (18 May 1986), 49ff.: *AAS* 79 (1986), 868ff.
11. Cf. Apostolic Letter *Euntes in Mundum* (25 January 1988): *AAS* 80 (1988), 935-56.
12. Cf. Encyclical Letter *Centesimus Annus* (1 May 1991), 12: *AAS* 83 (1991), 807-809.
13. *Gaudium et Spes,* 47-52.
14. *Lumen Gentium,* 1.
15. Cf. Apostolic Exhortation *Reconciliatio et Paenitentia* (2 December 1984): AAS 77 (1985), 185-275.
16. *Lumen Gentium,* 8.
17. *Unitatis Redintegratio,* 3.
18. *Unitatis Redintegratio,* 1.
19. Vatican II, Declaration on Religious Freedom *Dignitatis Humanae,* 1.
20. *Gaudium et Spes,* 19.

21. Tertullian, *Apol.*, 50:13: *CCL* 1:171.
22. Cf. *AAS* 56 (1964), 906.
23. *Nostra Aetate*, 2.
24. *Dei Verbum*, 25.
25. *Dei Verbum*, 2.
26. *Catechism of the Catholic Church*, No. 1271.
27. Apostolic Constitution *Fidei Depositum* (11 October 1992).
28. *Lumen Gentium*, 62.
29. *Lumen Gentium*, 65.
30. Encyclical Letter *Dominum et Vivificantem* (18 May 1986), 50: *AAS* 78 (1986), 869-870.
31. *Dominum et Vivificantem*, 51: *AAS* 78 (1986), 871.
32. *Lumen Gentium*, 7.
33. *Lumen Gentium*, 37.
34. *Gaudium et Spes*, 22.
35. *Lumen Gentium*, 13.
36. Cf. Paul VI, Encyclical Letter *Ecclesiam Suam* (6 August 1964), III: *AAS* 56 (1964), 650-657.
37. *Ecclesiam Suam*, 2.
38. *Gaudium et Spes*, 3.
39. Cf. Declaration of the Special Assembly for Europe of the Synod of Bishops, No. 3.
40. Cf. Encyclical *Redemptoris Missio* (7 December 1990), 37:AAS 83 (1991), 284-286.
41. *Gaudium et Spes*, 10.